Historic SHALLOW FORD *in* YADKIN VALLEY

Historic SHALLOW FORD *in* YADKIN VALLEY

CROSSROADS BETWEEN EAST AND WEST

MARCIA D. PHILLIPS

THE History PRESS

Published by The History Press
Charleston, SC
www.historypress.com

Front cover images: Price-Strothers map (bottom). *Library of Congress*; *Digital Davie* (top).

First published 2022

Manufactured in the United States

ISBN 9781467152907

Library of Congress Control Number: 2022937891

Notice: The information in this book is true and complete to the best of our knowledge. It is offered without guarantee on the part of the author or The History Press. The author and The History Press disclaim all liability in connection with the use of this book.

No one steps into the same river twice.

—*Heraclitus*

CONTENTS

PREFACE

This book is the biography of a small watery place called Shallow Ford. Since time before memory, it has been a natural crossing on the Yadkin River that became a stage for the changing fortunes of history. Then Shallow Ford vanished from sight during the last century When it was announced in the spring of 2021 that it had become the property of a conservancy and would become a historic site park, there was excitement among local outdoorsmen and historians. Rightly so, as this place had some really big stories to tell.

This is a labor of love for a place about which I knew too little before researching it. Fortunately, I am privileged to work as the keeper of the treasures in the Martin-Wall History Room at the Davie County Public Library and to have access to its great archives. As I suspected, the story lay hidden from view in files in plain sight.

Sources are credited within the text unless the information is in the realm of public knowledge; published sources can be found in the bibliography. If not in print, primary sources are available in local archives. The largest percentage of these, if not credited to another source, can be found in the Martin-Wall History Room. I spent many hours before and after work combing through a treasure-trove of letters, deeds and journals. They say that people become archivists so they can read other people's mail, and that is true. There is no better way to understand the common person's thoughts, fears and triumphs in another era.

This work is not an exhaustive treatment of any one of the events at or near Shallow Ford; rather, it covers a small area but many periods that require some backstory context. History does not happen in a vacuum, but rather in a linear cause-effect relationship with what went before and what came after. Stories must be told.

Shallow Ford is a very organic place, built by no man and subject to the forces of nature more than any man or government. There is something intrinsically authentic about a place where water has cascaded over rock for thousands of years. Man has crossed it but has little affected or altered it, while it changed the course of history. Thousands if not millions have stepped into its waters on the riverbank on one side and stepped out onto dry land on the other, mostly successfully, and it has never cost a cent to do so. Millions may have to be spent to create a park now to honor it. There is something beautiful about that tribute to this quiet but oh so special spot in the river.

ACKNOWLEDGEMENTS

No one works alone in history. Collaboration is the hallmark of local history, since its paper trail is never found in just one place (especially not in the folderol on the internet), but rather scattered in filing cabinets in local historical archives. Volunteers have accumulated bits and pieces of information, seemingly disconnected until someone comes along and connects the dots because the dots were provided. These are the facilitators without whom bits of local history would never find their way to the surface to be captured in the story where they belong. Local history is also found in the collective knowledge of local historians who have spent their lifetimes reading and taking oral histories down on the back of an envelope or trampling through murky places to find the place where history happened. I owe a great deal to these selfless warriors always on the search of the next important tidbit. Those who provided information that saved me immense amounts of time included Andrew Mackie, Ed and Sue Curtis, Dr. Gary Freeze, Merrikay Brown, Joel Reese, Robert Crum, Randell Jones and Jason Tomberlin. I am amazed how local historians are so eager that the story be known that they exercise little control over what they know. They share their secrets. What a special group you are, unacknowledged by the world but persistent in your pursuits. Nathaniel Philbrick calls these people who keep local history alive the "Fellowship of the Past." To all of you, who have welcomed me into your fellowship, Thank You.

Unpublished primary sources are the most reliable sources of history. The deeds, letters and photos in those file cabinets are like gold. First and foremost,

I owe a great debt to the Martin-Wall History Room at the Davie County Public Library. Some astute men and women before me, like Flossie Martin and James Wall, collected the vast pieces of information that can appear routine until that moment when they reveal that they are anything but. Local knowledgeable individuals shared what they knew with me freely, including but not limited to Marie Craig, George Haire, Gwynn Meroney, Cathy Veach and Charles Williams. Much appreciation for literary support from fellow author Randell Jones, lawyer and cousin Bob Bowers for clarifying legalities, brother extraordinaire George Dollar and splendid son Nathan Phillips for tech support and my brilliant daughters Dr. Annalisa Phillips Wilson for proofreading and Dr. Susanna Phillips for valuable suggestions.

Last but first, to Bill, who agreed to this endeavor knowing this time how consuming it would be and supported me at every turn, visiting sites, offering suggestions and bringing me food when I forgot to eat and was ignoring him. I know I could not do this without a good man as my husband. This is dedicated to you for providing me safe passage in life's crossings.

INTRODUCTION

Shallow Ford—such a simple name for such a complex place. The name describes the nature of the place but also its value to natives, settlers and even armies crossing the Yadkin River. Shallow Ford made an obstacle passable. That led to an array of crossings, from quiet pedestrian strolls to charging troops on horseback, eager explorers to animals pulling heavily laden wagons—they all got their feet wet at the same place. People crossed the river at Shallow Ford simply to get where they were going but in so doing, history was changed on those riverbanks.

History often happens in small places where no one is watching. Shallow Ford silently witnessed it, but that memory has now receded. Odd that Shallow Ford was much better known in the 1700s by word of mouth than it is in an era of mass media. Time and technology pushed it into the shadows.

Shallow Ford, and its significance, remains mostly unknown outside this immediate area. It does not show up in text or index of most history books that cover the Revolutionary War or Civil War. North Carolinians should take pride that this small place, now mostly hidden from view, was the pivotal point for so much of this region's history.

Is it possible that a path of wet rocks could turn people into Americans? The case can be made that the first self-determinaned Americans who mastered this vast continent may well have been Daniel and Rebecca Boone and their companions who pioneered the trans-Appalachian trail even as a new nation was being born. That critical journey through the Cumberland Gap began where they first left home and crossed a river. Shallow Ford was the place where the new rugged individualist American stepped into the water, committed to fulfill destiny. Then, 250 years of creating a nation followed and will soon be celebrated as its sestercentennial in 2026, including at a special place where destiny crossed a river.

So why did they cross the river? To get to the other side, of course.

SHALLOW FORD ON THE YADKIN RIVER

Before anyone crossed it, Shallow Ford was a place. A wide spot on the Yadkin River with bedrock stones, covered with gravel, laid naturally together stretching from the eastern bank to the western bank, it is more than just an embedded path to the other side of the flowing water. The Shallow Ford became a stage for human history.

Shallow Ford is strategically located on the Yadkin River just below where five sizeable creeks empty their waters into the swelling river, offering the combination of plentiful water, fertile soil and abundant wildlife to the pioneers it welcomed into the Forks of the Yadkin. It was as if it had been developing thousands of years for that moment in time.

A river provides water necessary for life but also poses an obstacle—separating someone from where he needs to be. Throughout history, travelers at the mercy of a fast river valued a safe crossing. A ford was quite simply a place where it was possible to cross a river safely.

Natural river fords were marked by several distinctions: easy access on both sides, not a forbiddingly fast current and, mostly, water that was not too deep. Crossing by foot, whether human or animal, is basically wading, less threatening in shallow water. Wagon wheels worked best if not completely submerged under water. Even horses shied away from deep water. So the key word in the name Shallow Ford is *shallow*.

A stable path under the water was a bonus. The Shallow Ford consists of a nearly level, solid rock base about one hundred feet wide that spans the river three hundred feet across diagonally. It is visible from the West Bend Bridge

Shallow Ford. *Keith Hall.*

just before the river bends out of sight, if the water level is low or if a heavy freshet has deposited flotsam on each side by the bank (debris trapped by the elevated rock bed at Shallow Ford).

A boulder on the western side of Shallow Ford called the Ford Rock was long a visible guide to the depth and safety in crossing. If the Ford Rock was not visible, the water was too deep and it was dangerous to attempt a crossing. No more than three feet deep was considered acceptable for crossing, but one-foot-deep water was ideal.

Safe crossings over rivers were such a necessity to identify and utilize throughout history that the concept snuck into culture in subtle ways. Death, especially a peaceful one, was often referred to as "crossing the river to the other side." The old spiritual "Swing Low, Sweet Chariot" resonated with, "I looked over Jordan and what did I see? Coming forth to carry me home—A band of angels coming after me." River crossing became symbolic of deliverance, if done safely.

Throughout much of history, the safe crossing concept had a more practical meaning. For instance, the two names most synonymous with higher education in the English-speaking world, Oxford and Cambridge, reflect this. Oxford was born as a Middle Ages location where oxen could ford the Cherwell River. When a bridge was built for humans and animals to cross the Cam River, the town of Cambridge sprouted on the riverbanks.

One of the most famous river crossings in American history happened on Christmas Day in 1776. General George Washington boated his troops across the Delaware River for a surprise attack on the Hessians in New Jersey, incapacitated by their celebrations. Made famous by artist Emanuel Leutze, the iconic image became engraved on the nation's collective memory even if it misrepresented the nature of the crossing. The icy river on that dark night made for a rough crossing, and indeed, two other boats were not able to make it. Washington would have never stood up in the boat as depicted (not to mention the flag not yet designed). Washington was familiar with the dangers of river crossings. In 1777, before Lafayette arrived to assist the American Revolution, Du Coudray, the highest-ranking Frenchman serving the Continental army, drowned when his horse was spooked and jumped off a ferry crossing the Schuylkill River. Later, when President Washington toured the South, the horses pulling his carriage also leaped into the water of the Occoquan River; after difficulty, they were unfastened and he was saved. The reality of frightened horses was so common that they would be unfastened to save the other riders in case they took a fright and jumped off the ferry.

Shallow Ford was for centuries one of four major fords on the Yadkin River stable enough for animal-drawn wagons, stagecoaches or military cannons. This rare stable crossing place became a thoroughfare. The other major ford on the Yadkin River that could support wagons was the aptly named Trading Ford near Salisbury. However, Trading Ford was prone to being unpassable and dangerous at times. Benson Lossing, in his illustrated *Field Book of the Revolution*, described the Trading Ford in the Revolutionary

Washington Crossing the Delaware. Library of Congress.

War as a "row of stakes that then stood there to guard the stranger from the deep water below." Cornwallis's guards would yield to the wooden guards on a night in 1781.

In a very private place and without anything like a tollbooth, no one knows exactly how many people crossed the Shallow Ford, but what is known indicates that many more crossings took place than show up in any historical record. Even surviving ferry records only represented paying users, and nonpaying travelers continued to walk across the ford simultaneously. Arguably hundreds of thousands, and perhaps millions, walked through the water at Shallow Ford over several centuries.

In addition to fords, multiple ferries existed along the Yadkin River, particularly in the nineteenth century, including one at Shallow Ford ran by Orman Kimbrough. His 1825 record book in the Davie County History Room shows a busy schedule and a reasonable fare of seventy-five cents for a wagon crossing. Why even have a ferry crossing that close to the Shallow Ford? Physically, ferryboats could navigate deeper waters than crossing on foot and simplify cargo crossing. Economically, the free ford was always the affordable option for the poor. Ironically, in the 1800s, there were many more ferries facilitating shortcuts across the river than there are bridges today.

The Yadkin River's significance may not be readily apparent in a passing glance from the West Bend Bridge far above the water. Part of the larger Yadkin–Pee Dee River Basin, the Yadkin River's tributaries and branches cobweb across the Piedmont landscape it makes fertile. The Yadkin River is the life-supporting system of nourishment that makes human habitation possible in this portion of North Carolina.

The story of the Yadkin River is not just what has happened on it but rather its own story—where it begins, travels and ends on a daily basis. The Yadkin originates in the higher elevations in the mountains, makes its way through the Piedmont and, as the Pee Dee River, eventually to the Atlantic Ocean at Georgetown, South Carolina.

For thousands of years, water has coursed downhill from the mountains. Crevices between rocks became gullies and then ravines as the dynamics of heavy downpours and spring thaws farther upstream made the Yadkin River a fast current.

The Blue Ridge Mountains soar above the western landscape of North Carolina and drop down significantly to the Piedmont in a geographic escarpment. This dramatic shift in altitude means meandering creeks cascade as waterfalls into ponds that become forceful rivers.

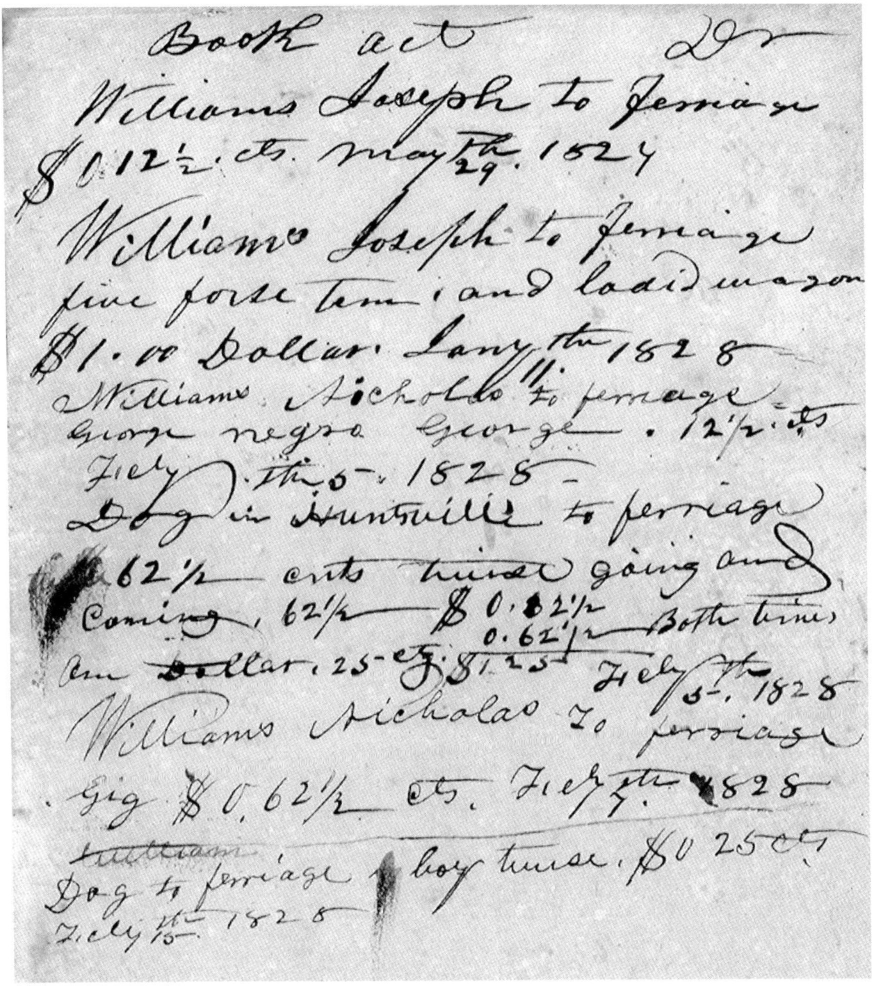

Book act Dr
Williams Joseph to ferriage
$0.12½ cts. May 29th 1824
Williams Joseph to ferriage
five horse team and loaded wagon
$1.00 Dollar Jany 11th 1828
Williams Nicholas to ferriage
George negro George . 12½ cts
Feby 5th 1828
Dog in Huntsville to ferriage
62½ cents twice going and
Coming, 62½ $0.62½ Both times
0.62½
One ~~Dollar~~, 25 cts $1.25 Feby 5th 1828
Williams Nicholas To ferriage
Gig $0.62½ cts. Feby 7th 1828
~~William~~
Dog to ferriage boy twice, $0 25 cts
Feby 15th 1828

Kimbrough's ferry account. *Martin-Wall History Room.*

These mountains are part of the greater Appalachian Mountain Range, which is much longer than most people imagine. The Appalachian Mountain Range spans the eastern North American continent from central Alabama north to the Canadian province of Newfoundland and Labrador. Geologically, the Appalachian Mountain Range extends to a rocky tip on the easternmost edge of Belle Isle, Newfoundland, before disappearing undersea into the Atlantic Ocean. It surfaces briefly on a peninsula in Greenland and then reemerges as the highest cliffs on the western coast of Ireland, known as Slieve League in Donegal, making it one very long mountain range.

Like many rivers, the Yadkin begins as a bubbling spring on high ground. Today, that source is buried under a parking lot outside the Green Park Inn Hotel in Blowing Rock, directly across from the entrance to Blowing Rock. The river's origin is unmarked and barely discernable under a rusty grate. The headwaters of the Yadkin, almost imperceptible through the grate, immediately disappears under a road and then emerges a few feet later through a culvert as a trickle southward alongside Highway 321.

The Yadkin River is edged onward by rock boundaries in a southerly and then easterly direction, slowed down by the W. Kerr Scott Dam in Wilkesboro built in 1962 to temper the floods, until it reaches the Sauratown Mountains, where the path of least resistance forces it through a gap. This abrupt directional change south is called the Great Bend.

The river then flows 135 miles, gathering strength in volume and widening, past Pilot Mountain and Winston-Salem and between Salisbury and Lexington until it marries the Uwharrie River to become the Pee Dee River. The Yadkin River comes to an end in name where the Pee Dee River begins but contributes it water to a greater flow.

One admirer of the Pee Dee River was composer Stephen Foster. After a visit to a plantation on the river in South Carolina, he wrote the lyrics to "Old Folks at Home," with the opening line "Way down upon de Pee Dee River." The publisher liked the sound of "Swanee River" better, and the Pee Dee vanished from making musical history. It became the state song of Florida in spite of the fact that Stephen Foster never set foot in Florida or saw the Suwanee River there. It was the waters of the Yadkin and Pee Dee that had inspired him.

For a long time, it was hoped that the Yadkin River could be made usable for transporting commerce. Farmers were convinced that such a large river had to provide a watery avenue for big boats carrying their crops to market. The first of three organized attempts to make the Yadkin River navigable from Wilkesboro to the coast was begun as early as 1785.

Revolutionary War hero Richmond Pearson and fellow locals Andrew Hunt and John Johnston were commissioned by the Rowan County Court to determine what dredging, dams and canals could make this possible—alas, with no success. However, they did not give up, and men began to buy up land, including Major Peter Hairston, who purchased the 2,500-acre Cooleemee Hill plantation from Pearson at a prime location on the river.

In 1818, a second attempt was made to make the river navigable by the Yadkin Navigation Company. Benjamin Latrobe, famous surveyor and architect of the U.S. Capitol, was recruited to draft a design for the company.

Right: Yadkin River origin. *Courtesy of author.*

Below: Bean Shoals wall. *Digital Davie.*

Within a few years, the investors had spent $85,000, with only one retaining wall to show for it at the Bean Shoals.

A final attempt was made in 1847 when it was proposed to send small barges down the river, pulled by steamboats. Completion would have required several canals to be built to circumvent difficult spots.

In the end, Hairston had to transport his tobacco by wagon to Richmond but managed to keep his plantation, while the other investors ended up deeply in debt. So confident were the investors that land was laid out for the port town of Clinton in the forks of the Yadkin. Lack of success and a looming war doomed the project finally by 1860. The Yadkin River never became a commercial waterway and served the people of the Piedmont.

The notion of the Yadkin River reaching the ocean did not die easily however. A 1938 April Fools' joke in the *Twin City Sentinel* in Winston-Salem fooled locals. A front-page story reported that a transatlantic steamer had "plowed through the muddy waters of Yadkin River and anchored 10 miles west of Winston Salem." A doctored photo seemingly showed it. Even though the article made it clear that it was a prank, after the paper hit the streets at noon, old Highway 421 was jammed with cars going to see this phenomenon on the Yadkin. All they found was the usual lazy river. It simply is not possible for a large boat to come that far inland on the Yadkin River.

The Yadkin River has flowed constantly for thousands of years. Just when man first stepped into its waters went undocumented, but the river would wash millions of feet at Shallow Ford.

NATIVE AMERICANS

A white man observed, "Hard by the Savanna's we found the Town, where we halted; there was not above one Man left with the Women, the rest being gone a Hunting for a Feast. The Women were very busily engag'd in Gaming: The Name or Grounds of it, I could not learn, tho' I look'd on above two Hours. Their Arithmetick was kept with a Heap of Indian Grain." Thanks to explorer John Lawson, Europeans and their descendants were exposed to this aspect of native lifestyle. It was a hard life dependent on the land and elements, but while the warriors were off hunting, the women made time for a game. This new world on the verge of being claimed was full of surprises.

In the six hundred years before the arrival of Europeans, the Native Americans have been identified as being in the Woodland Period, where tribes began to stay in one location rather than being migratory. There are archaeological traces of gardens and the cultivation of crops, indicating a desire to live in one place. Unfortunately, the smaller tribes in the Piedmont were less inclined to do this because they were less powerful. Without stockade defenses, a settlement with gardens and grain stores was easy pickings for more powerful tribes.

The Woodland Period is also marked by the increased use of pottery shards found at archaeological sites. Throughout the world, pottery serves as a reliable artifact for dating a site. While consistently made from clay, pottery changed rapidly in small ways, like designs, the marks of ever-evolving tools and even added composites. Once a piece is identified, it can indicate a time frame in which it was created. Early Woodland Period pottery was basic, mostly shaped for cooking. Later pieces show evidence of more specialized function, better quality and even artistic decoration.

Local knowledge of Native American presence has been greatly enhanced by the work of twentieth-century archaeologists. When Highway 421 was being constructed in the 1950s and widened in the 1970s, archaeologists from the North Carolina Department of Archives and History were often barely ahead of the bulldozers as initial digs revealed many native sites in the Piedmont. The earlier excavations mostly recovered human remains at burial sites, whereas the latter uncovered more pottery.

The Donnaha excavation in 1973 by Wake Forest University along the Yadkin River uncovered hundreds of thousands of broken bits and pieces—ceramic, stone, bone and shell artifacts. Nineteen burial sites and numerous refuse pits were uncovered. Missing were posts or other foundational supports linked to the building of homes. The majority of the sites hugged the river. One notable exception is the Hunting Creek site—there the remains of a concentrated settlement are on a hilltop about 1,500 feet from the nearest water source.

Five fishing traps (called weirs) built by the Indians still remain intact in the Yadkin River north of Shallow Ford. A weir is an intentional obstruction of stones to channel fish into a trap. Five extant ones close together tells us that the Indians had found a good fishing hole and gathered there.

The natives showed the Europeans how they carved canoes out of the "tall trees" along the river named "Yatkin" by them. No doubt natives paddled canoes across the strip of rock that crosses the Yadkin River called the Shallow Ford. Unfortunately, insufficient historical record exists for future generations to appreciate their story.

There were four major language groups or families among the native groups, and three of them were local—the Siouans in the Piedmont, including the Saponas, Tutelos and Catawbas; Algonquins to the northern and higher elevations; and the Iroquoians in the higher mountains, including the Cherokees and, to the east, the Tuscaroras.

"The story of the Native American was told by early European explorers, not themselves," as Dr. Gary Freeze has noted. Practically the only historical account prior to settlers in the Yadkin Valley comes from the 1714 London publication of Lawson's *History of North Carolina*, written by a curious, articulate British man about whom very little else is known. John Lawson arrived in the Carolinas in 1700. On December 28, one day after his twenty-sixth birthday, he launched the journey of more than five hundred miles mostly on foot, beginning in South Carolina and then crossing into present

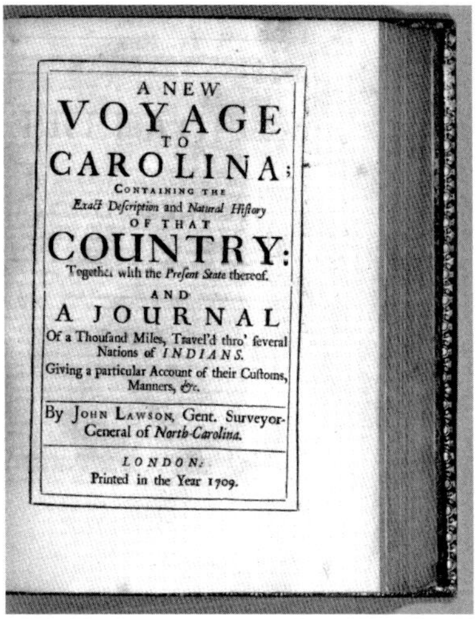

John Lawson's book. *Courtesy of author.*

North Carolina, in an arc that took him north and west before swinging through the Piedmont. His account of native tribal life, animals and plants is a fascinating read that should be required reading for every North Carolinian. How else would moderns know about the games native wives played when the men were away?

While it is difficult without definitive landmarks to determine exactly where Lawson wandered, local territory is recognizable when he described a "Tract of Land lying betwixt the Inhabitants and the Ledges of the Mountains, from whence our noblest Rivers have their Rise, running toward the Ocean, where they water as pleasant a Country as any in Europe." Mentions of "Pleasant Savanna grounds" viewed from one distinctive mountain (Pilot Mountain probably) with "delicious country" along a river as wide as the Thames, lined with tall trees and with "curious bold creeks" emptying into it, might well describe the land along the Yadkin River. He described the land on one side as "mountainy" and put into print for the first time the name "Appalatche."

Larson wrote of mostly fertile soil but on the far side of the river described ground he compared to "Marl," an old English word for extremely hard clay. Local buck tallow, or bull tallow, certainly fits this description. This apt account of the Piedmont means that he probably crossed at Shallow Ford, one more path his guide, Enoe-Will, would have led him down.

Lawson reported on various trees, such as the persimmon tree, an old heritage type still growing locally. He described it as "if eaten before [ripe], draws your Mouth up like a Purse, being the greatest Astringent I ever met." The animals and insects he richly listed (including chiggers) are still recognizable to residents. He told of watching a technique the Indians used to dry venison, a cooking style he called "barbaku"—no translation needed.

John Lawson interacted with tribes known by the names they gave themselves, including the Saponas and the Tutelos. The Saponas were a small group later absorbed into the stronger Catawba Indians. The smaller tribes united in their fear of the Cherokees in the mountains. When he called the indigenous people "savages," Lawson was using the terminology of his day, but he also noted their noble ways. He mentioned intriguing customs and observed that he never saw a left-handed native. Treated by them as a friend, he felt safe until he encountered the Tuscarora tribe, which brutally murdered him.

Nomadic people groups historically moved themselves and their animals to the resources rather than be tied to one spot. The natives shared the natural world with no tradition of individual ownership. Tribes controlled areas for their own use, but a written deed was a foreign concept. The natives protected access to resources, while most of Europe's wars were fought over borders on a map. The natives' future would change dramatically as they were pushed off land that they had only occupied and not owned on paper.

The Cherokees were still fur trading allies with the French when the French and Indian War broke out. The westernmost colonists were easy targets. After a lull of several decades of Indian attacks, the settlers found themselves threatened. A number of settler families, including the Boones, relocated mostly back into Virginia, returning to harvest their crops while others stood guard. In June 1760, Jonathan Hunt of Bryan's Settlement told the Moravians that over half that community had fled elsewhere.

By 1761, the Cherokees had been beaten back and sued for peace, and the worst conflicts with the natives in the Shallow Ford area were past. A smallpox outbreak in 1759 had reduced the native tribal population to a mere five hundred, down from tens of thousands. A century of resisting white advancement had failed for the original inhabitants. In the next century, the Cherokees would face one final decimation in the Trail of Tears but they were already defeated by then. There is still no word in the Cherokee language for "goodbye"—perhaps because they did not understand the desire to leave. But leave they did, in a slow exodus west and north, with some tribes ending up in Canada. The last full-blooded Tutelo-speaking native, named Nikonha, died at age 105 in 1870 so the colonial era was the beginning of a long goodbye for these natives.

At a disadvantage in weaponry and immunity, ultimately retreating from the white invaders became the natives' only recourse. They would be absorbed into the new nation, given land that was then taken away and removed onto reservations. It remains one of the darker chapters in the American expansion story.

Remarkably, in a practice known as the warrior tradition, Native Americans have participated in the U.S. military in every war in which the United States has fought. They continue to defend their land, wearing the uniform of their adopted country.

PIONEERS AND SETTLERS

When Daniel Boone got the itch to relocate his people to better hunting grounds, he explored the Florida Panhandle and bought land. Then he came home to the cabin on Sugar Tree Creek near Shallow Ford and excitedly described it to his wife, incidentally mentioning swamps, reptiles and mosquitos. Rebecca listened and no doubt they talked late into the night after the children were fast asleep. History changed course after those muffled discussions, but not in Florida. Rebecca refused to move her children to that environment so Daniel considered another direction, looking west. While it can be hard to comprehend settlers who would uproot their households and lives to start over in uncharted territory, that conversation of a young couple by a dying fire resonates still. She would not go there and he would not go without her. Rebecca was not stubborn or unwilling to relocate with her husband, as she would many times. After all, she was of pioneer stock but the option Daniel offered simply did not suit her. Brave as the early settlers were, the challenge had to appeal to them. And there were risks to weigh. They were not simply launching out willy-nilly into any unknown land but would do so in a carefully chosen one. That human element is critical to remember in what was about to unfold at Shallow Ford in the mid-1700s.

Europeans came rushing into the Piedmont, not in a trickle but in a flood, not as explorers but as settlers. Newcomers brought packhorses and wagons, loaded down with household supplies. All roads led to Shallow Ford, the ford that could support this throng, the colonial equivalent of the Thames River of boat travel, the Grand Central Station of train travel and the Atlanta Airport of air travel. Anyone moving around the Piedmont of North Carolina area simply had to get across the Yadkin River, best and most frequently done at Shallow Ford.

Shallow Ford became a landmark to a new frontier—"west of the Yadkin" referred to a new territory. The land was different in its nature from the older eastern part of the colony and hosted a unique lifestyle. The beginning of westward expansion would captivate pioneers and chart the next century of American history. The Yadkin Valley was the first Wild West, waiting to be tamed.

By 1720, those who had found refuge in Pennsylvania from religious persecution and overcrowding in the old world of Europe began to feel a bit crowded in the new one. They simply wanted more land. The European practice of primogeniture kept large estates intact so only the eldest son inherited land. Since it was never divided, there were never small tracts of land available to buy. Having been denied landownership in Europe, the draw of owning land and controlling their own fates was the pull of the push-pull of human migration. Seeing their name on a deed was something of which the descendants of medieval peasants could only dream.

Migrating pioneers coming down through the sloping open lands of Virginia and into the Carolinas found ever-widening open land. The Appalachian Mountain Range encroaches closer to the coastal areas in the north but gradually fans out farther west in the south. They found more tillable land before being confronted by challenging mountainous terrain. The land literally got bigger the farther south a pioneer traveled in eastern colonial America.

These dreamers spilled down a path that quickly became the most traveled road in the colonies, the Great Wagon Road, with various names along the way. The Great Philadelphia Road began as Market Street in Philadelphia, one block from Benjamin Franklin's print shop, and took pioneers west across Pennsylvania until the mountains blocked their way. Heading south through the Shenandoah Valley, it was known as the Carolina Road. In the Carolinas, it became the Georgia Road, as that was the next goal, but many settlers never made it that far, deciding to stay in the rich land in the Carolina Piedmont.

Much debate has ensued about the exact route of the Great Wagon Road in present North Carolina. Remnants show up where the heavy wagons on it caused the dirt to become so packed down that it is still hard to plow. Leaving Virginia, the road snaked its way through present Stokes and Forsyth Counties. Traces of it between Pilot Mountain and Bethabara

Great Wagon Road pioneers, artistic rendering. *State Archives of North Carolina.*

show up alongside modern straightened versions on Stanleyville Road where wide, elongated ditches serve as a palimpsest of the colonial road. The Great Wagon Road then curved southwest and navigated the spiny ridge that rises above the Yadkin River to the east of Shallow Ford.

Reliable sources indicate that the Great Wagon Road crossed the Yadkin River (as it had to somewhere) at Shallow Ford. On the west side of the Shallow Ford, after the path rose up, there was an immediate parting of the road, with one path going west and then southwest to the current Georgia Road that slices through the southernmost corner of Yadkin County and reemerges in Davie County by the same name briefly. The name of the pieces of that puzzle tell the whole story—it was channeling settlers toward Georgia.

The other road that separated within mere yards of the Shallow Ford on the western riverbank makes an abrupt turn to the north, into the Old Mulberry Fields Road. This initial path is on private property now, but it is possible to stand in the V where the road divided and where settlers chose the direction fate would take them in life.

Someone had to be first. The earliest recorded pioneers who arrived immediately west of the Yadkin River in proximity to the Shallow Ford were George Forbush and Morgan Bryan (two of their children married so they climbed onto the same family tree). The settlers' story unfolded with Morgan and Martha Bryan and their family, the ones who first tilled the land nearest Shallow Ford in the Forks of the Yadkin.

Morgan Bryan, the first pioneer in the Shallow Ford area (his name has been often misspelled as "Bryant"), was not a young man but seventy-seven years old when he chose this last great adventure in a life already marked by many. Morgan was born in Denmark in 1671, his Irish family having escaped the ire of Oliver Cromwell when his grandfather opposed him. Morgan grew up in Ireland after his father returned to retrieve family lands and titles, but it was not to be. Seeking his own fortune, Morgan left Ballyroney, in County Down in Ireland, and landed in the Roanoke Settlement in Virginia at age forty-eight.

Bryan married the much younger Martha Strode there and their journey together began. The next thirty years gave them nine children and the wherewithal through land speculation to take yet one more leap of faith: leading a large extended family into the Forks of the Yadkin. Little could Morgan Bryan have known that his children would settle the yet unexplored Kentucky west of the mountains in the coming fifty years. Bryan family historian John K. Bryan Jr. aptly described Morgan's story as "a veritable saga of the early American frontier."

Bryan followed no white settler to this new place and as the first, he had to literally blaze the trail. The Great Wagon Road was far from Great at that point—it was hardly even a road, let alone one that wagons could survive. It was a rocky trail through Virginia, with multiple rivers to be crossed safely. Obstacles like downed trees and fallen rocks, for a stretch along the Virginia/North Carolina border, made the path sketchy and disappear altogether on maps of the time. Bryan cleared stretches of the path that then became a heavily traveled road, briefly referred to as the Bryan Road in Virginia.

The large extended family of Morgan Bryan loaded up and left Virginia after harvesting the summer crop to realize its profit. Their journey was three hundred miles long and took three months but no one on this exodus got sidetracked; they arrived in the Forks of the Yadkin intact on November 29, 1748, just before winter.

Bryan had the means to secure thousands of acres of land in various parcels and, unlike most settlers, did so before clearing and planting it. His land speculation paid off handsomely; many ancestral lands in the area began their deed chain as belonging first to him. His primary "sales" were to his children (for twenty pounds each regardless of when they came of age), seven sons and two daughters and their husbands, including son-in-law William Linville, who helped him survey the land. (Linville is memorialized in name at a waterfall and gorge in the mountains where he and his son were later killed by Indians.)

While Bryan purchased land elsewhere, the bulk of his holdings were identified by family historian John K. Bryan Jr.: "The heart of the settlement described an arc across the northern half of the present Davie County and the southeastern part of what is now Yadkin County, North Carolina. On the East, the arc anchored on the North Fork of the Yadkin…just south of the 'Shallow Ford' of the river across which passed the road between Wachovia and the new Rowan County seat of Shallow Ford." The reference to Wachovia is a later one because Moravian journals first described inspecting their new claim in 1752 by referencing Bryan's Settlement. He beat everyone, even the Moravians, into this part of the wilderness, and his land became their landmarks.

Bryan's Settlement was more than just a landownership designation; it became the early name of a sprawling community that dominated the western shore of the Yadkin River near Shallow Ford. Today's Farmington was first called Bryan's Settlement and then later Little Currituck for settlers from the coast before George Wesley Johnson called it Farm Town, which the United States Post Office changed to Farmington.

Morgan Bryan's landholdings were extensive but his homeplace was on the largest tract just west of Shallow Ford, near the current Sparks Road, according to Kathryn Weiss. Morgan built what was called the Mansion House, a large log structure on a sizeable plantation. Daniel and Rebecca Boone's home in a cabin on Sugar Tree Creek, where they lived the longest in this area, was no doubt part of Morgan Bryan's original holdings. Rebecca was Morgan and Martha Bryan's granddaughter so they were living on family land.

Morgan Bryan also designated in writing on deeds a portion as "Martha's Land" for his wife. Her name appears far more frequently in land deals than most colonial women. Even though she was much younger than him, Martha died a year before Morgan died in 1763 at the age of ninety-two. The patriarch and matriarch of this large clan were buried on their own land, as was the frontier custom. Their graves are believed to be under a tennis court in the Oak Valley subdivision in Advance now. A marker nearby unceremoniously marks the place and its neglect. Martha's tombstone was rescued and is in the holdings of the Rowan County Museum.

The family Morgan Bryan had brought south was just beginning to make their mark in history. Rebecca and Daniel Boone would soon lead another mass family migration of Boones and Bryans, this time directly west.

Rebecca Bryan Boone—of whom no likeness exists and who, reportedly, did not even know how to read or write—was a sharpshooter who often hunted to feed their family when Daniel was off on extended hunting trips. This pioneer woman, who first crossed the Shallow Ford at age nine in that massive Bryan cavalcade, became the primary physical link between the first settlers west of the Yadkin, the Bryan family, and her husband, Daniel Boone, who led settlers, including her and their children, into the Great American West. The concerned mother by the fireside who hesitated became the critical link between the Forks of the Yadkin and the rest of the western development of the American nation. In an era when women were perceived to be powerless, this intentional woman was anything but.

This frontier in the Yadkin Valley of North Carolina did not just predate but actually gave rise to the western frontier beyond the mountains. Arguably, the Forks of the Yadkin was the first such western frontier in American history, as well as the training ground for the next. While populations had hugged the eastern coast for a century and a half, the Carolina Piedmont was among the first locations for a deliberate surge into a place just for a land grab. If the Forks of the Yadkin was the first western frontier, it almost immediately became the launch pad for the next chapter and then many others to come.

Clinton Weslager wrote, "America was settled by restless people." The cause/effect relationship between the Forks of the Yadkin and the western frontier was that the Carolina frontier prepared pioneers for the next one. The first western pioneers could not have come straight out of Philadelphia or Boston or even Charleston. Instead, they arose armed with the skills necessary to conquer a new land after being shown by their fathers how to do it. The Great Wagon Road would first lead settlers to the gateway at the Shallow Ford, from where Daniel Boone would launch his explorations into Kentucky; the future of America lay waiting beyond it.

Land-hungry settlers quickly followed the Bryans into the Carolina Piedmont. In 1751, Irish immigrant and acting governor Matthew Rowan wrote of the throng surging into where would soon be a county named for him. Only fifteen years later, Governor William Tryon stated, "I am of opinion this province is settling faster than any on the continent, last autumn and winter, upwards of one thousand wagons passed thro' Salisbury from the northward to settle in this province chiefly; some few went to Georgia and Florida, but like it so indifferently, that some of them have returned." The first "halfbackers" (a modern nickname for northerners who first retire to Florida but then relocate back halfway in the Carolinas) had arrived by 1765.

On the other side of the Yadkin River from the Bryan settlement, the Moravians landed and began making many contributions to local history, not the least of which was their journal keeping. As a missional people, they saw divine purpose in everything they observed and began daily recording it. In this as-old-as-time practice, humans tend to record in written form what they witness God has done, bringing a significance to otherwise daily routines of life. As a practical resource, these Moravian journals are a wealth of information about the colonial era. They even recorded the weather. The journals were written in German but two centuries later Miss Adelaide Fries translated this mammoth work into English. Colonial history in this area profits greatly from their attention to detail.

The prolific Moravian journal writers made frequent mention of the Bryans and the intriguing, strong friendship with their neighbors. After Moravian missionary Georg Soelle died in 1773, missionary Richard Utley made a five-day journey around the Bryan Settlement reading multiple accounts from Soelle's memoirs to various members of the Bryan family, including an early trip by Soelle, when he had "crossed the Atkin; spent the night with Morgan Bryant" and many others.

The first individual settler to own land immediately east of Shallow Ford was Samuel Davis, who arrived in 1752 and almost immediately sold the land where one descended into the water at Shallow Ford to Edward Hughes, who then owned the land on both sides of the path to the ford on the eastern bank. Hughes recognized opportunity and in 1753, he applied for and was granted a license to open a tavern where he would live and serve travelers crossing Shallow Ford for the next fifty years. Shallow Ford became his home.

Edward Hughes was not just an opportunist but a bit of a scoundrel, participating in a lot of fights and initiating a few. He insisted to the official land agents that he had paid for some of the land the Moravians developed when all records indicated otherwise. Worse yet, he was charged with misappropriation of public funds, found guilty and sentenced to serve time. However, when he was elected sheriff of Rowan County in 1758, his sentence was suspended until after he completed his term of office. Land sale records in the next century indicate that Hughes may have lived to be over one hundred years old, when the average life expectancy in 1800 was thirty-six years of age.

By 1753 (five years after Bryan's arrival), Rowan County had its first sheriff, a sure sign of law and order. Without a courthouse, business was often conducted in a home or a public house (pub). The first sheriff, David Jones, lived on his 220-acre farm that adjoined that of Samuel Bryan, in the Bryan Settlement. Jonathan Hunt of Huntsville was one of the justices of the county court. Squire Boone (whose home was once referred to in an official document as a pub, probably for this reason) served as justice in temporary courts of law. Rowan County was a massive county but law and order was maintained locally near Shallow Ford.

The Cape Fear Road was built to link the Moravian town of Salem with Cross Creek and coastal trade items came up and over the ford to the western settlements. All this commerce created taxes, and when trouble brewed in Cross Creek (now Fayetteville), news also traveled along the road to stir up the protests that resulted in the Regulators War.

To the west of Shallow Ford, old roads included one that trailed off to the northwest, down the old Mulberry Fields Road through present Yadkin County, toward Wilkesboro. A second road went directly west to Huntsville and closely aligned to the current Huntsville-Courtney Road. A third road veered off to the southwest into the stretch called Georgia Road off Wyo Road and then again in Davie County.

Notably, no road turned immediately south directly along the Yadkin River, no doubt due to the land occupation by the Bryan family. July 1762 saw authorization of cutting the Irish Ford Road, so called because it led from Huntsville south to Salisbury, a settlement of mostly Irish settlers. It is Farmington Road now, a few miles west of and loosely parallel to the river.

Population growth generated surveys, which also tell a story. Two young surveyors were commissioned to survey territorial boundaries that would become the road map for the next generation. Peter Jefferson became well known for surveying western Virginia and naming features like the New River, but his greatest fame would be as the father of his seven-year-old son at home named Thomas, future author of the Declaration of Independence and president of the United States. The other surveyor was Joshua Frye, first commander of the Continental army in the early days of the Revolution. En route to Fort Duquesne, he fell off his horse and died from his injuries. Another young surveyor by the name of George Washington quickly replaced him in command.

The Jefferson-Frye Map of 1751 shows the Great Road taking settlers across the Potomac and then descending into the valley of Virginia. By the time a newer edition was printed in 1775, it was labeled "The Great Wagon Road from the Yadkin River through Virginia to Philadelphia distant 435 miles." In four years, the perspective had shifted to the emphasis being on the Yadkin River, not the Potomac. The updated map included the community of Bethabara and then crossing the Yadkin River directly to the west. The map is not precise in topographical details, but the only road from Bethabara west at that time went directly to Shallow Ford, the only obvious and logical choice for the Great Wagon Road crossing.

While the Great Wagon Road has disappeared, interest and claim to it has not. Kyle Stimson researched and made the case for the Great Wagon Road's course through Forsyth County, but local communities still debate claims to the most famous road in colonial America. What all proposed routes of the Great Wagon Road share in common (besides some confusion about exact location) is the crossing at Shallow Ford. On a map such as the 1808 Price-Strother map of North Carolina on the cover (the new state's first), Shallow Ford appears like the center focal point from which not only the Great Wagon Road to Georgia but also other developing transportation routes spin outward.

Many a journal written in colonial times by travelers included entries about having to wait for the water level to go down at the ford in order for the crossing to be safe. At Shallow Ford, camps of those waiters developed on both shores. When the Ford Rock was completely submerged, it was too deep for a safe crossing. Time to make camp and watch a rock.

Traffic shifted from pedestrian to wagons of households being hauled around by settlers. The tavern licensed to Edward Hughes proved that travel on the road was increasing. Inns, or taverns, sprang up to accommodate travelers. They traditionally provided liquid refreshments, food and a place to lay your head. It was not unusual for a small room at an inn to be crowded with as many beds as would fit and rented to as many men as could fit in a bed. This was not Comfort Inn. It was a place to rest one's head and hope that the bedmates were small boned. It must have beaten the alternative of sleeping outside on pine needles, as these inns did good business, an oasis of sorts in the wilderness.

From the Shallow Ford, the next inn down the Great Wagon Road was on the corner of Georgia Road and Bear Creek Church Road in present Davie County. John Pinchback had a license to operate the Pinchback Tavern there, charging the rates mandated by local law for meals and overnight stays, but for one pence more, the sheets on the crowded bed could be clean ones. Inns also served the needs of the settlers whose homes began to pop up along the Great Wagon Road. An inn became a gathering place in a community where news and newspapers could be obtained from travelers. Inns also hosted lively political debates and the occasional fisticuffs.

One portion of the Great Wagon Road was so called because the transportation of choice quickly became the newly designed Conestoga wagon, created in the Conestoga Valley in Pennsylvania. It was a large, sturdy

Nissen wagon ad. *Martin-Wall History Room.*

covered wagon, perfect for transporting a family and their goods (many local residents treasure heirlooms brought by their ancestors in one). It also was bow shaped like a boat, so it could be floated if necessary (although it would have been too heavy unless unloaded first). Large iron wheels carried the wagons that could be made as big as twenty-six feet long and eleven feet high. To make unloading easier, the hinged tailgate was added (pickup truck owners benefit from that innovation). Another improvement for long hauls was a board over the left front wheel for the driver to sit on; drivers began sitting on the left side and driving on the right side of the road.

The Conestoga wagon sold for $250 and was destined to take Americans south and then across the mountains and continually westward to the Pacific coast. A century later, locally made Nissen wagons were still being advertised in local newspapers. Travelers not moving households used stagecoaches, so called because horses had to be changed out at stages of a long trip, creating the need for blacksmiths. Mail coaches soon followed, establishing the line of communication that would continuously bring others to the frontier.

The New World offered physical mobility instead of the elusive class mobility of the Old World. Having relocated once, these immigrants were not going to settle for the first place they saw. They would look a bit longer before squatters became settlers. Whole families packed up and agreed to start over again and again. This would become a theme in American settlement, no doubt frustrating some housewives who had just planted gardens.

Land was getting limited in the mid-Atlantic colonies. Unlike today, where hundreds of people live in a square mile, then it took hundreds of acres for a farm to support one family. The communities in Pennsylvania became overcrowded with an influx of Europeans in the early 1700s. Scarcity, as always, increased the price of land, making it less affordable than it had been to the previous poor immigrants. Between 1713 and 1732, the cost of land in Pennsylvania had multiplied sevenfold per acre.

Many ethnic groups had found sanctuary in the colony of Pennsylvania, known for founder William Penn's generous hospitality. Two of these groups, dissimilar in many ways but alike in their desire for land, found themselves traversing the Great Wagon Road together and both stopping in the Carolina Piedmont. The Scots-Irish came first in their impulsive, rowdy way and the Germans followed, the Moravians having taken time to overthink, pray and cast lots about it. Evidence of this order of arrival is, as Robert W. Ramsey observed in *Carolina Cradle*, that all the creeks have English and not German names. However, these two groups became the physical and cultural gene pool of descendants still living where they landed.

The Scots-Irish from the Scottish borderlands by way of Ulster and the Germans by way of Moravia were from totally different cultures in the Old World. The fighting Scots-Irish rebels were untamed, reckless rustics. The Germans were far more refined in everything from their music to building traditions. Scots-Irish brought homemade Celtic stringed instruments to create bluegrass tunes and built log cabins. The Germans managed to bring brass instruments (an early Moravian brought little baggage with him, but it included his trombone, possibly the first in this hemisphere) and wrote classical hymns to be performed on pipe organs in tall brick buildings. Compare Whippoorwill Village in Wilkes County with Old Salem, the Moravian site in Forsyth County.

What these contrasting groups shared was a tortured past, persecuted for their beliefs and discriminated against in complicating ways. Hampered in worshiping differently than that of the ruler of the land where they lived, their passion to find a place where they could be free to live and worship as they wished drove them to find the same place in North Carolina.

Having been forced out of their original homelands by politics mixed with discrimination, these two pioneer groups became known by places they retreated to first—Moravia and Ireland. Both were misnomers. (Furthermore, names like Dutchmans Creek still reflect the confusion between the German Deutsch and the Dutch.)

The Scots-Irish label came with an added indignity. Often referred to as Scotch, not Scots or Scottish, and Irish as an addendum, this people group were neither Scotch nor Irish. In America in the nineteenth century, Scottish immigrants were called Scotch, like the drink, a slur suggesting they were mostly drunken and lazy. And they were Irish only briefly after the British government forcibly relocated Scots from along the troublesome borderlands with northern England to northern Ulster in Ireland. So the Scots-Irish were accustomed to relocating before they chose to flee to America and were already resentful of the British telling them what to do. Fiercely independent, they preferred to be left alone, but if not, they would fight at the drop of a hat. This desire to control their destiny had been a long time in the making.

The Scots-Irish (as well as those who came directly from Scotland and Ireland) brought old habits to the New World. They were inclined to be "squatters" on properties. They had no problem with claiming land that was not occupied and defied anyone to move them off. Land deeds were a government technicality they might or might not get around to later, as they were never inclined as a rule to accommodate governments. Neither did they like paying taxes or rent. In all fairness, their families never had experience in owning land or the costs associated with that. As Robert W. Ramsey wrote, they "were by no means a group of destitute encroachers. Most of those who avoided payments of taxes and quit rents seem to have been unwilling, rather than unable, to pay."

Inclined from past experiences to know that any dwelling might be temporary and not on land they owned, they built small makeshift shelters, using the logs in great abundance in the American landscape. The word *cabin* comes from the Scottish word *cab* or *cabbin* for a small structure, basically a hut. One-room structures, cabins were built from what was available—stone at their feet in the Old World or the heavily wooded terrain in the New World. Even the common size, approximately sixteen feet long, came from an old Scottish measurement called a rod.

While Germans also built log homes, the Germans in Wachovia built mostly sturdy brick and stone block buildings, still standing. It was the Scots-Irish who threw up log cabins as temporary housing, a notion born in the Old World where they had known housing insecurity.

John Boone cabin. *Digital Davie.*

Historian David Hackett Fischer wrote of the ways British immigrants shaped American culture in a fascinating book called *Albion's Seed*. One folkway he describes was the Scots-Irish impact in the western Carolinas. Philadelphia merchants wrote in 1717 how the number of ships jumped dramatically, loaded with this new group from the border counties of Scotland/England. They had relocated south by the midcentury, not as individuals but families, not wealthy but poor and not humbly but with a stubborn pride inconsistent with their circumstances. They were a jolt to the colonial Brits. Fischer wrote that the Scots-Irish immigrants "brought to America an indelible memory of oppression which shaped their political attitudes for generations to come." They called the frontier a "dark and bloody ground," as their history had prepared them to think all places were.

The Scots-Irish's story was a long one of conflict. The travails of William Wallace and Robert the Bruce were only one short chapter in nearly seven hundred years of the fight over the English borderlands and Scotland. The expression "dying with their boots on" arose out of this long-standing war that made its people stubborn and combative. Trusting only their own gave rise to clans with chieftains and Highland games that celebrate old fighting methods. Men trained and lived as warriors, while women worked hard on their farms to compensate for the head of the household who was often gone off fighting.

Even their speech gave their history away. One legacy of the Scots-Irish is what linguistics reveals. The dialect of the backwoods Scots-Irish in America includes traces of Elizabethan English that persist in a form more concentrated than anywhere else in the world, even modern England. This Shakespearean tongue shows up as the tendency to drop the *g* at the end of words like *coming* ("She'll be comin' round the mountain when she comes").

The Germans congregated in clusters with strong communal bonds. The Scots-Irish preferred to go, as Daniel Boone said, where no smoke from other cabins could be seen. The first was socially dependent and the other fiercely independent, yet they have coexisted in the Piedmont ever since. Whether to intentionally create a church community like Wachovia or like the Boone family to escape the condemnation of the Quaker church that ostracized them for marrying out, new frontiers meant no established institutions telling one how to believe and live. Appreciation of that was something the Germans and the Scots-Irish shared.

Scots-Irish were tough Presbyterians, followers of John Knox, who had so frightened Mary, Queen of Scots, that they became immortalized in the nursery rhyme Little Miss Muffet. When a famine struck Ireland, the flight to escape resulted in 12,000 people per year coming to the American shores. By the 1750s, more than 200,000 Scots-Irish had come through Philadelphia, one third of all the Scots that had been in Ireland before this great exodus. Europe was emptying out its most troubled people and they were jostling for places in a new world.

The Germans arrived next, close on the heels of the Scots-Irish. They landed in small clusters like the Heidelberg community in present Davie County and built the Heidelberg Lutheran Church (mistakenly called the Dutch Meeting House) circa 1760. The congregation had disappeared by 1871, when the property was sold, with the proceeds used to build a stone wall around its cemetery, its last vestige today.

One exceptionally large German group arrived near Shallow Ford on the east side of the Yadkin River as a highly organized church family. The Moravians were a reformation group that dated back to the martyr Jan Hus. Not Lutherans, as most Germanic kingdoms were, they had been forced to seek asylum in the old kingdom of Moravia, where Count Nicolaus Zinzendorf gave them land, protection and a zeal for missions. He himself traveled to the island of St. Thomas and was one of only a few European nobility to visit the colonies. The Moravians relocated as the guests of the British government and William Penn to Bethlehem, Pennsylvania.

Moravian bishop August Spangenberg then purchased land in the colony of North Carolina that was just shy of 100,000 acres and just east of the Yadkin River, called Wachovia after the beautiful Wachau Valley. They began at Bethabara, near the Great Wagon Road, while they built the town of Salem as a trades town for the greater area. Wachovia became six Moravian communities, all controlled well into the 1800s by the ruling body of the church. Ultimately, the German-speaking Moravians became English-speaking Americans, absorbed into the local community but maintaining a deep sense of their history.

An interesting phenomenon marked the colonial mass migration into Piedmont Carolina. They came as families rather than single men, looking to create familial security. Their combined finances bought larger plantations, and they stuck together, as would some of their children when they jumped over the mountains, moving literally lock, stock and barrel. Family was the priority, but not tied to one place as in Europe. American mobility began in the 1700s, not to escape family ties but to give security to them.

Pioneers like Charles Hunt, Abraham Creson and Squire Boone flooded the Forks of the Yadkin and obtained land grants. The town of Huntsville steadily developed at a natural crossroads where travelers and locals crossed the Shallow Ford, traveled down the roads leading away from it or settled close by.

A telling statistic is that by the mid-1750s, three men had requested a license from the new court in Salisbury to run a ferry across the Yadkin River—Benjamin Rounsavill at Trading Ford, Isaac Feree (a homophone for his trade) for an unidentified location and Edward Hughes at Shallow Ford. Increased traffic prompted increased means of crossing.

Before these pioneers came south, the colony of North Carolina had been molded by royal actions across the ocean in London. In 1728, seven of the eight Lords Proprietor of the Carolinas sold their holdings back to the Crown after sixty-six years of proprietorship rule, a sweet deal of selling back what had been given them. It had not been a particularly profitable arrangement for the proprietors. Indeed, the wrangling over rights and responsibilities involved the proprietors' legal secretary, John Locke, who, due in part to the dilemmas created in the Carolina colony, wrote *Two Treatises on Government*, widely read by the Founding Fathers in America and studied still on the concept of government as a social contract.

When the British king wanted to reclaim the land his ancestor had given away, only John Carteret, Earl of Granville, wanted to keep his. King George II struck a deal with Carteret in 1746 that in essence gave a swath of North Carolina to one man in a rectangle sixty miles wide across the northern border with Virginia to Coldwater Creek. Granville had an advantage in the royal court as the rare landed gentry in England who spoke German, the king's first language (after the death of childless Queen Anne, the British had adopted the German Hanover rulers as their own—it was not one of the happier adoptions in history).

Commissioners surveying the western portion of the colony in 1746 stopped at the Haw River, slightly southwest of Cary. They refused to go farther because there was no one to the west who might provide food and supplies. Morgan Bryan arrived two years after that, and thirty years later, when the War for Independence began, the Granville district was well populated.

Matthew Rowan surveyed the land that would be named for him. Granville never saw his land, but his control would last until neither the English king nor any earl ruled there. In 1777, North Carolina, flush with the freedom the Declaration of Independence had announced to the world, passed the Confiscation Act, boldly claiming all the lands owned by the Crown or other British subjects not already claimed by settlers. The Granville District became the spoils of war, and the winners were the pioneers with their names on those Granville Land Grants, one of the best land deals in history.

Also in 1746, King George's men defeated the Scottish Highlanders at the Battle of Culloden in a final way that determined that the brutal Scottish fighters were no match for the organized British army. To get rid of the leaders not executed, the remaining captives had their sentences commuted to transportation to the American colonies. So in the same year that the land deal was sealed for the Granville District, many Scots were given free transport to America. It only got better for the losers.

Only one year later, settlers began to flock from northern colonies. Word traveled fast. By 1753, more than one thousand settlers were in the area that became Rowan County. Having almost no white residents in 1746, Rowan County quickly became one of the most populated counties.

Those land grants do not make sense in the modern American mindset of landownership. Basically, Granville's land grants traded the right to live off his land in exchange for closing costs and the settler's promise to pay an annual quit rent. The British colonial government also demanded property taxes. As many as 640 acres, approximately one square mile, could be obtained in a single grant, but a person could apply for multiple plots as long as they paid the initial fees and taxes. It was like winning the lottery to families who had never known such an opportunity.

The deeds to these grants used the word *indentured*, not *sold*, on them, as it was a contractual agreement, basically a perpetual lease on the land, harking back to the fiefdom of the Middle Ages. The word *indenture* came from a medieval practice of indenting or perforating a line in the middle of the legal document so the contract could be torn in two identical halves; each party had one by which to hold the other responsible. For example, a 1761 Rowan County deed to Isaac Wilcoxson for 320 acres stated that the contract was for an "Indenture" to him and his heirs "forever" for the cost of ten shillings in sterling with an additional twelve pounds required in yearly rent.

Earl Granville was a generous landlord, encouraging his agents to show "indulgence" to a tenant unable to pay the quit rent because of a misfortune or poverty. He was also patient with tenants who waited as long as five years after getting a survey to complete the application process in order to postpone rents.

One effect of this cheap land was that settlers whose names appeared on early grants often quickly disappeared from local records. Selling land was pure profit under these circumstances, so many sold and moved on to new land. Others snatched up grants as speculators, always intending to sell. Wealth was unnecessary as only initial fees were required.

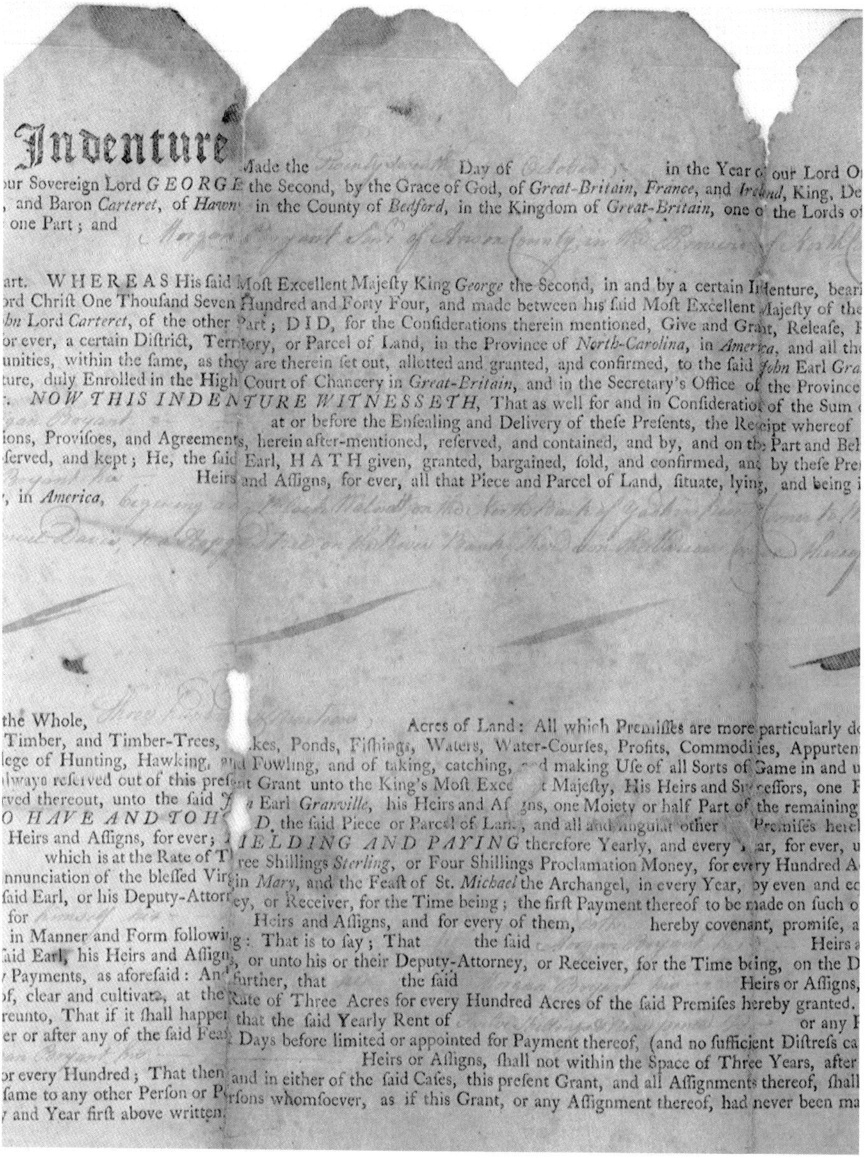

Indenture Made the Day of in the Year o our Lord O
our Sovereign Lord GEORGE the Second, by the Grace of God, of *Great-Britain*, *France*, and *Ireland*, King, De
, and Baron *Carteret*, of *Hawn* in the County of *Bedford*, in the Kingdom of *Great-Britain*, one o the Lords of
one Part; and
art. WHEREAS His said Most Excellent Majesty King *George* the Second, in and by a certain Indenture, beari
ord Christ One Thousand Seven Hundred and Forty Four, and made between his said Most Excellent Majesty of the
hn Lord *Carteret*, of the other Part; DID, for the Considerations therein mentioned, Give and Grant, Release, F
or ever, a certain District, Territory, or Parcel of Land, in the Province of *North-Carolina*, in *America*, and all th
unities, within the same, as they are therein set out, allotted and granted, and confirmed, to the said *John* Earl *Gra*
ture, duly Enrolled in the High Court of Chancery in *Great-Britain*, and in the Secretary's Office of the Province
. *NOW THIS INDENTURE WITNESSETH*, That as well for and in Consideration of the Sum
at or before the Ensealing and Delivery of these Presents, the Receipt whereof
ions, Provisoes, and Agreements, herein after-mentioned, reserved, and contained, and by, and on the Part and Bel
served, and kept; He, the said Earl, HATH given, granted, bargained, sold, and confirmed, and by these Pre
Heirs and Assigns, for ever, all that Piece and Parcel of Land, situate, lying, and being i
, in *America*,
the Whole, Acres of Land: All which Premisses are more particularly d
Timber, and Timber-Trees, kes, Ponds, Fishings, Waters, Water-Courses, Profits, Commodities, Appurten
lege of Hunting, Hawking, and Fowling, and of taking, catching, and making Use of all Sorts of Game in and u
lways reserved out of this present Grant unto the King's Most Excellent Majesty, His Heirs and Successors, one F
rved thereout, unto the said *J* Earl *Granville*, his Heirs and Assigns, one Moiety or half Part of the remaining
O HAVE AND TO H D, the said Piece or Parcel of Land, and all and singular other Premisses here
Heirs and Assigns, for ever; *IELDING AND PAYING* therefore Yearly, and every ear, for ever, u
which is at the Rate of Three Shillings *Sterling*, or Four Shillings Proclamation Money, for every Hundred A
nnunciation of the blessed Virgin *Mary*, and the Feast of St. *Michael* the Archangel, in every Year, by even and ec
said Earl, or his Deputy-Attorney, or Receiver, for the Time being; the first Payment thereof to be made on such o
for Heirs and Assigns, and for every of them, hereby covenant, promise, a
in Manner and Form following: That is to say; That the said Heirs a
aid Earl, his Heirs and Assigns, or unto his or their Deputy-Attorney, or Receiver, for the Time being, on the D
Payments, as aforesaid: And further, that the said Heirs or Assigns,
of, clear and cultivate, at the Rate of Three Acres for every Hundred Acres of the said Premises hereby granted.
reunto, That if it shall happen that the said Yearly Rent of or any F
er or after any of the said Feast Days before limited or appointed for Payment thereof, (and no sufficient Distress ca
Heirs or Assigns, shall not within the Space of Three Years, after
or every Hundred; That then and in either of the said Cases, this present Grant, and all Assignments thereof, shall
same to any other Person or Persons whomsoever, as if this Grant, or any Assignment thereof, had never been ma
and Year first above written.

Bryan land grant. *Martin-Wall History Room.*

The Granville Land Grants spurred the growth of Rowan's county seat, Salisbury. Irish Presbyterians populated Salisbury and infused it with their culture, like the Knox family, who were related to John Knox who tutored King James I of England (whose authorized translation of the Bible in the

English language became a standard for centuries). James Knox Polk, the grandson of the Knox family pioneers to Rowan County, would become the eleventh president of the United States.

Granville's land agents were responsible for having the land surveyed. The surveyors recruited the local "squatter" to help carry the chains and he made sure the boundaries were right. The land also had to be registered and producing taxes to be paid.

Lord Carteret, Earl Granville died on the second day of the year in 1763; when word reached Rowan County weeks later, grants were already in process. Hence there are surviving documents that supposedly Lord Granville signed on the day of his death, one might say virtually, and the surveys were completed months after the fact. In the previous fifteen years, more than seven hundred grants had been made in this part of the Granville District.

One people group came not of their own choice: slaves. Originally indentured servants were brought to the colonies as menial workers, but once they earned their freedom, they left to claim their own land. The solution to this dilemma was slavery, as that was for life. Slavery was not common on the frontier, to a large degree because it was not settled by those wealthy enough to own numerous slaves. Nonetheless, it was an increasing reality for farmers and merchants to own a few and became common practice to loan and trade slaves between them.

About 7 million African slaves were brought to the British colonies in North America during the 1700s. In North Carolina, the Black population mushroomed from 6,000 in 1730 to more than 40,000 by 1767. The greatest increase occurred just prior to the Revolution, mostly in the plantations of the East. In the developing West, fewer than 10 percent owned slaves. Rowan County knows the names of the first two Black people to arrive in 1747, as twin enslaved brothers Paul and Saul drove their master Adam Sherrill's livestock across the Catawba River.

Private Roy E. Wilson, who served his country. *Courtesy of the Wilson family.*

While slaves did not come of their own will, their descendants stayed, made it their home and richly contributed to its culture. Like Native Americans, African Americans have defended their adopted country in every military action in U.S. history.

REGULATORS WAR

In the small Sandy Creek Baptist Church building set in pastoral surroundings, around the corner from Regulator Herman Husband's farm, Elder Shubal Stearns advocated for nonviolence to church members when hundreds gathered at an association meeting in 1769, admonishing them that they should not take up arms against the government. Four armed Regulator leaders on the grounds responded by immediately charging into the church sanctuary, challenging him. That day, the faithful witnessed the showdown between a small militia and a lone preacher in his pulpit.

Elder Stearns's response to their demands to support their more violent demands for their rights was not recorded, no doubt because those who would ordinarily take notes were too stunned to do so. It was remembered that he was soft-spoken and evasive, not words normally used to describe this preacher. Known as a man of strong speech accompanied by his famous piercing eyes, this revealed a very human side of a pastor, no doubt concerned for the safety of his flock. He likely thought it wise to not fight back, but instead humbly diffused the situation in the hopes of steering violence away from the church. (Violence did happen when a church at Haw River reinforced his directive; opposing Regulators demanded the members' rifles, even breaking into their homes and severely beating one member.) Stearns decided not to argue with brethren with whom he disagreed, and rather than dictate to his hearers and divide the attendees into two warring sides, they had to decide for themselves the right thing to do. In the annals of church business meetings showdowns, this one was high drama.

Sandy Creek Baptist Church. *Randolph County Historic Landmark Preservation Commission.*

Stearns was perceived as weak by some, but he did not run and he completed the preordered items of business in the meeting. As always, there were hotheads and cooler heads among the group pressing for change. By the time the Regulators War was finished, more than 90 percent of Sandy Creek Baptist Church's members had relocated for safety, so a price was paid. There would be a physical battle before it was over, but it would be on a battlefield near Alamance Creek and not in a church sanctuary at Sandy Creek, the sanctity of which one man had humbly protected.

How had a disagreement over taxes come to a potential gunfight in a church sanctuary? The relationship between Britain and its colonies had deteriorated in the backcountry of North Carolina.

The Granville Land Grants brought thousands into the colony of North Carolina, but they came with taxes, imposed by a government far removed and offering no benefits to frontier settlers. While the battle cry "no taxation without representation" was still a few years off, the idea was rooted in the frontier of the Carolina Piedmont. Rough and about-to-be-ready backwoodsmen protested the violation of their rights and appealed to their king, whom they trusted to protect them.

However, the king's emissary, Governor William Tryon, was deeply hated. He became the focus of a struggle that would be the beginning of the end of the worldwide British empire. Many historians claim that the American Revolution's first military conflict was the Battle of Alamance, between the British-supported eastern government and the Regulators. The break with the British would have happened eventually in New England, but in typical backwoods style, North Carolinians did not wait for that. Often perceived as backward, the settlers who resisted government control in the 1760s were forward thinking, foreshadowing and leading the charge for independence.

Given their history in the old country, the backcountry settlers did not have the loyalty to London that the eastern descendants of direct transplants did. The Scots-Irish had fled oppressive English control. The Germans had no relationship at all with the British royalty. Few held allegiance to a British landlord. And carving an existence out of a wild frontier had empowered them to think for themselves. Being anti-whatever-was-the-political-norm was the norm of the frontier.

London changed the rules on the settlers and began to enforce laws long relaxed or ignored, particularly in increased taxes used to pay the hated royal governor, supply his troops and pay off the debts from the French and Indian War. Various taxes randomly soared for unknowable reasons. A letter in the Colonial Records of North Carolina from Abraham Creson of Shallow Ford told a tale of a widow: The local clerk asked her about her means. When told she had been left well off, the clerk promised to charge her extra taxes. Marriage taxes jumped from the equivalent of one to fifteen dollars, and many weddings never showed up in the official records as a result. It was very arbitrary, and the royal clerks were hated for lining their own pockets as well as putting off poor engaged couples and mistreating widows.

Furthermore, cash was scarce in a barter economy on the frontier so taxes, which had to be paid in currency, were particularly burdensome and colonial taxes were disproportionate. Poll taxes were the same for the poor as the rich. Failure to pay could result in their land claim being auctioned out from under them.

The westerners were not fairly represented in the colonial assembly either. One-third of the population under Governor William Tryon's tenure was located in the western counties, but they were represented by only eight of the seventy-two assemblymen. The eastern counties feared control by the fast-growing population in the west, and the assembly reluctantly added new counties to avoid being outnumbered. Western settlers struggled not only with the faraway British Crown but also the eastern government of their own colony. It was Carolinians against Carolinians.

A fight was brewing. The first mention of the Regulators movement was in the Bethabara Diary for September 23, 1758. Earl Granville's chief surveyor, William Churton, told of a meeting: "The mob, about 700 strong, had formulated its demands into certain Articles. One Article demanded that the Vestries should be abolished and that each denomination should pay its own ministers." Vestries were taxes parishioners paid for the Church of England and vicar. This hit particularly hard people who attended Protestant churches that had sprung up in opposition to state churches.

The "mob" was a peaceful assembly of dissenters who had drafted their grievances in writing. The main issue was being taxed to support ministers of the established Church of England, which they did not attend, nor could they as there were none yet in the west. (When Governor Dobbs died, a justice of the peace had to conduct his funeral as no official Church of England minister could be found.) Other pastors could not legally conduct weddings.

Governor Tryon called the Regulators a "faction of Quakers and Baptists" and the Baptists "avowed enemies of mother church." When a Church of England clergyman was sent to Rowan County, he complained that the "Anabaptists" were being married by their own preachers, denying him the marriage fee.

Then Governor Tryon levied yet one more unreasonable tax to build a stately Government House in New Bern, known still as Tryon's Palace. He lived in it one year. Tryon's Palace burned down in 1798, but its reproduction serves as a reminder of a costly residence, the final straw on the backs of backwoodsmen who lived in log cabins.

The protestors consisted of poor farmers concentrated in the Piedmont counties. This power struggle between eastern control and western frontiersmen also became a test in the relationship between the British ruler and his subjects. While Governor Tryon ultimately won in this contest of wills, the trust was destroyed London would mistakenly count on Loyalist support in the Revolution that had eroded during the Regulators movement in the western frontier of the Carolinas.

The year 1766 saw the public reading of an announcement organizing citizens in the colony to resist unfair taxes. There was a meeting called to air grievances, then another and another and another. They called themselves Regulators based on a British term for reformers, but these were rowdy reformers. John Sparks observed, "The present reputation given to Appalachian natives as being rustic, backwards, impulsive, ignorant and violent hillbillies possibly had its beginnings in the Regulator conflict during this very time."

The first organization of the Regulators happened at the farm of Herman Husband, neighbor to Elder Shubal Stearns. Husband hailed from Maryland, was converted under George Whitefield's preaching and was a conflicted Quaker who sometimes attended Stearns's Baptist church. Sparks accurately described Husband as "one of the most complex, bizarre personalities to ever dance across the stage of North Carolina—or for that matter, American—history." He worked for a land company but fancied himself a scientist and philosopher and was a lifelong correspondent with

Benjamin Franklin, believed to be his source for the politically charged pamphlets he distributed. Later, he participated in the Whiskey Rebellion, while mapping out what he called the New Jerusalem in the mountains.

The Regulators did not see themselves as rebels but as defenders of the principle of the Magna Carta of 1215—that kings ruled to protect their subjects' rights. They hoped that if His Majesty was made aware of abuses, he would right all wrongs. So, throughout the conflict, the Regulators appealed and petitioned, even though they were repeatedly disappointed.

In 1768, the Moravians recorded in their diary that "on the Yadkin a number of settlers met at the home of Isaac F[e]ree and signed a contract against the Public taxes and other grievances." Shallow Ford residents were hearing the news from passersby and participating, signing a commitment to the issues and one another. While that particular petition is not known to exist, others do as humble appeals to the king they still trusted with their welfare. A few weeks later, a Moravian missionary who had traveled to preach to a group near Shallow Ford wrote that he found them all elsewhere at a political meeting about the issue of unfair taxes. The wildfire was spreading.

While Shallow Ford residents were entering the fray, Governor Tryon had Herman Husband arrested. Regulators near Hillsborough surrounded the prison where he was held, protesting that a farmer who simply met with other farmers and signed appeals should not be incarcerated. No laws in which they believed had been broken. They were not wrong.

The governor's man on the scene, Edmund Fanning, attempted to pacify the crowd by approaching them from the far side of the Eno River, with a bottle of wine in one hand and a bottle of rum in the other. He asked for a horse to be sent over so he could join them and negotiate a truce. The gruff Scots' response from the other bank was "Yer none too good to wade!" And there the talks broke down. It was not only one of the strangest river crossing encounters of the era but also a statement that the farmers could not be bought, at least not by someone unwilling to ford a river by foot, no matter how much booze he was totin'.

Tryon marched across the Piedmont with his militia in full uniform, fully armed. He was on a mission to recruit and make a show of power. It is uncertain whether he crossed the Yadkin River at Shallow Ford or Trading Ford (maybe the latter since a recruiting event was held in Salisbury), but regardless, Tryon intimidated the common people of the Yadkin Valley. When Governor Tryon surrounded the Hillsborough jail like a fortress, the Regulators slipped away during the night in order to avoid armed conflict.

The protestors avoided a physical fight as long as possible. Herman Husband was found not guilty in court and set free. He ran for a seat in the assembly and won.

The Regulators would push back in other ways. Farmers who had struggled to pay taxes even while protesting them decided to withhold them, in an "extralegal" way (words Marjoleine Kars used in *Breaking Loose Together: The Regulator Rebellion in Pre-Revolutionary North Carolina*), to get attention to their grievances. They also upset the election of the vestry, the governing body that collected taxes for the Church of England in Rowan County. Two local Presbyterians led them along with a Baptist preacher from the Shallow Ford area, Pastor Joseph Murphy of Timber Ridge Baptist Church. The Anglican minister in Salisbury, Reverend Theodorus Drage, wrote to Governor Tryon that Murphy "talks away, seducing the people." These three men put forth a list of candidates for the vestry who would not collect the hated tax. They won and even occupied the courthouse until midnight on the last day the vestry election could be challenged. Their battle cry was "everyone should pay their own clergy." Maybe not the most catchy or famous fighting words, but they had succeeded in winning the battle legally without physical fighting. Thirty years later, Thomas Jefferson would coin the phrase "separation of church and state" in his letter to the Danbury Baptists in 1801, but long before that, men in Salisbury in 1770 had sorted it out.

The summer of 1770 also produced the most severe drought anyone could remember in the Shallow Ford area. When it rained at the end of August, it poured. Rivers were so flooded that not even ferries could run, and a wagon overturned at Shallow Ford, costing a life. Travel and the ability to assemble were severely affected, and history was stalled by the high rivers.

When the assembly finally gathered in January 1771, Governor Tryon pushed through the Riot Act Law, retroactive to the Hillsborough protest. It ruled that any gathering could be deemed a riot and participants could be arrested and tried. The assembly also created four new counties in order to weaken the Regulators' base, including Surry. Husband was expelled from the assembly and imprisoned under house arrest in New Bern. So afraid was Tryon that he had guards posted to watch the guards on Husband.

In May, Piedmont farmers assembled on a field near Alamance. The Regulators had come for a discussion, bringing only guns and ammunition needed to hunt for their food. Governor Tryon arrived accompanied by a thousand troops, six swivel guns and two cannons. Dynamics had dramatically shifted. The two camps had a bit of a standoff for several days.

The Regulators sent a petition to Tryon asking for a hearing. In response, Tryon moved his troops closer. In a second appeal to the governor, three men, including a Presbyterian minister, asked for a hearing. Tryon took them hostage, sent one back with the obvious answer and the command to disperse in one hour. Then he shot one of the messengers in front of the crowd.

When Tryon demanded that the Regulators appear before him or be charged as traitors, they maneuvered hoping to avoid armed conflict and then requested, one last time, an audience with the governor. He responded that he would only agree to it if they lay down their arms, which they perceived as a trap and would not do. Tryon ordered them to disperse or they would be fired upon.

Herman Husband had shown up, hoping to arbitrate a settlement, but when fighting broke out, he fled the scene, remembering his lapsed Quaker pacifism. He escaped to Pennsylvania under the assumed name of Tuscape Death (for good reason, as he was the only leader never pardoned) and only reemerged under his real name after the Revolution was over. He left the Regulators without a clear leader even as a battle they had tried to avoid began.

That day at Alamance, battle ensued, and the Regulators had the initial advantage as they shot from behind trees at the British soldiers lined up in traditional European military fashion. That quickly changed when ammunition ran low since the protestors were not well armed. Then Tryon had the woods where the regulators were fighting set on fire. The battle lasted less than two hours as the surviving Regulators fled for safety. Twenty Regulators were killed to nine of the governor's men. Several were arrested and Regulator James Few, a twenty-four-year-old new father of twins, was hanged on the spot.

The day after the Battle of Alamance, Tryon held a kangaroo court and condemned a dozen men to death. Captain Messer's ten-year-old son begged to be hanged in his father's place as his mother lay crumpled on the ground, distraught. The governor reportedly said, "Your father will not be hung today"—that final word proving crucial. Governor Tryon offered Messer his freedom if he could capture and bring back Herman Husband, the movement's leader. Messer tried and almost succeeded in capturing him, but because the governor was holding his family as guarantee, he returned empty-handed rather than escape. Then Tryon hanged him.

Governor Tryon then went on a revenge trip, beginning with destroying Husband's farm and that of Benjamin Merrill in the Jersey community near Trading Ford. Merrill had led a group of three hundred men toward Alamance but turned back when he learned that it was a battle and not a protest any more. No matter—Merrill was ripped out of his bed and taken prisoner. Abraham Creson was arrested on his farm north of Shallow Ford, and they searched for Pastor Joseph Murphy there, in vain. Other Regulators fled for their lives, some to the mountains. It was said that locals were afraid to hide or feed them but would leave bread out on a post so they would not starve along their escape route.

Governor Tryon then marched his captives through the Piedmont, no doubt across Shallow Ford, in a week of drenching rain, in order to terrorize others. He offered a pardon to any who would surrender their guns and take an oath of allegiance. Many tough conversations around kitchen tables resulted in 6,400 men taking the terms and the pardon (about three quarters of the free males in the area). Their names on petitions had become death sentences.

Tryon took his prisoners to Hillsborough, taking time to destroy the farm of the parents of James Few, whom he had hanged at Alamance. On June 13, William Tryon received word that he was being transferred immediately to New York but told no one until he completed his final act as governor, rushing the trial of his prisoners two days later. He had the gallows ready and trees cut down so family and friends of the condemned could watch the execution. Of the twelve leaders he arrested and tried, he freed six, and the others were taken to the gallows. There Benjamin Merrill, in the presence of his wife and ten children, spoke of his peace with his God and quoted a Psalm before being hanged.

The hanging of Merrill and the torching of his family's house and lands left a stinging reminder in the Yadkin Valley. A deacon in Jersey Baptist Church, Merrill was greatly respected in the community. Traveling preachers for years visited his widow to encourage her, but she never recovered from the trauma. Tryon tried to make an example of Merrill, but he became a martyr in local eyes. Two of Merrill's sons would fight with the Patriots in the Revolution.

Abraham Creson of Shallow Ford was tried for treason but released. Thousands more Regulators fled to the mountains. The fire for freedom had not been extinguished but simply scattered. This is the story told in the dramatic production *Horn in the West*, the saga of Boone and other towns where disillusioned settlers could retreat and hide. Particularly hard hit were Baptist churches. Morgan Edwards, Baptist historian, estimated that as many as 1,500 Baptist families moved away, looking for a place they could worship, taking Baptist beliefs into the new frontier. Sandy Creek Baptist Church shrank from 600 members to 14 in a year after the Battle of Alamance.

For one small church in Little River and another about to be born near Shallow Ford, the response of attendees to the advice of Elder Stearns was game changing. Pastor Joseph Murphy, himself supportive of the biblical position of not attacking government leaders, possibly had been at the Sandy Creek meeting and witnessed that famous showdown. Little River church members were more committed to fighting for the Regulator cause than he, and rather than cause a church fight over it and hurt the name of the ministry in the community, Murphy quietly departed for another group of believers in need of a pastor. The place was called Shallow Ford because of its proximity to the well-known river crossing. Within a year, the group of believers and its new Pastor Murphy would organize as Timber Ridge Baptist Church and soon exchange meeting in members' homes for a structure, a meeting house. It would become the first Baptist church west of the Yadkin River.

Although it was well known that there were Regulators, including member Abraham Creson, in the Shallow Ford area who would continue to participate in the conflict, apparently this small congregation would treasure peace over political posturing. But that was not the end of it for Murphy. He was still on a list as the pastor of the pro-Regulator church at Little River and they knew after the battle where to look for him, living near the crossroads at Shallow Ford. Traugott Bagge, Salem's shopkeeper, observed Tryon's soldiers searching for Pastor Murphy but reported that they were unable to locate him. Some said that he hid out, protected by the Bryans. Local legend was that he hid in Boone's Cave on the Yadkin River, where Daniel's family had supposedly camped. Murphy did write later that the troops stole his papers and a new pair of stockings, the only things of value in his modest cottage. Murphy revealed these events to Morgan Edwards but never where he had hidden, perhaps thinking that he might need that secret again.

Most significantly, when the North Carolina Constitution was written in 1776, thirteen of the forty-seven sections reflected reforms first proposed by the Regulators. The Regulators War represented a seismic shift in power—it would no longer work vertically, top down, but horizontally, between peers. A uniquely American idea had been born in the backcountry. The freedom fighters lost the only battle but would soon win the war.

AMERICAN REVOLUTION

Richmond Pearson was part of the stream of pioneers when as a nineteen-year-old he came to the Yadkin Valley. Twenty years later, he was a lieutenant in the militia company commanded by Captain Samuel Bryan of Bryan's Settlement. There was just one glaring problem. Pearson was a staunch Patriot and Bryan was a Loyalist. When called to muster for duty, Pearson did the honorable thing and resigned his commission instead of falling into rank. Bryan refused to accept it. So, there at Veach's Muster Ground (now in Liberty Methodist Church's cemetery in Davie County), they agreed to settle their differences in a gentlemanly way: with a fistfight. They fought it out, probably first posturing and stepping around each other with fists raised and by the end wrestling on the ground, to determine for whom the militia would fight (or so legend says). Lieutenant Pearson won, and the militia joined him to harass Cornwallis. Captain Bryan decently went his way to assist Cornwallis. Torn apart by conflicting loyalties, the residents in the Forks of the Yadkin went to war. Like the other colonists, having begun with noble posturing, they would soon be down and dirty on the ground.

The War for Independence was never a foregone conclusion. Having been British colonists and mostly loyal subjects, many wanted to maintain the status quo. Others were buying into the ideas filtering down from New England about inalienable rights. So some fought to defend the king, others to sever ties with him and some wished that the fight would not happen at all. There was no making everyone happy, so fight they did.

Veach's Muster Ground location. *Digital Davie.*

Much of what Americans know about the American Revolution is encumbered with two misconceptions. First, the emphasis has always been on the war in the North, in cities like Boston and Philadelphia. Little attention was paid to south of the Mason-Dixon line. For the first five years, the participation of the South seemed like an afterthought and therefore less important. The British government itself was sluggish in fighting in the South. British strategists had always counted on stronger loyalty and support among the southern colonies and strategized accordingly. They seriously miscalculated southerners as well as their landscape.

Secondly, identifying the conflict as a "revolution" is a misnomer. Technically, a revolution is where a group overthrows its existing government and replaces it with a new one, as the French did in their revolution, albeit a few times too many. The American War for Independence was not a revolution because the American colonies never attempted to overthrow King George or Parliament or replace either. They wanted to separate and be left alone, more of a civil war at first and then a war between two nations after the Declaration of Independence. The conflict should be accurately called the War for Independence. But Columbus mistakenly called the natives "Indians," and millions have perpetuated that error, as well as calling the war for independence a revolution. These accidents of history have staying power.

Just as confusing can be the names by which the conflicting sides were and still are identified by historians. The newly minted Americans and their troops became known as Continentals or Patriots or Whigs. Those colonists who wanted to remain British citizens were called Loyalists or Tories. The names Whigs and Tories stemmed from British politics, where Tories believed in royal rule and Whigs preferred being at the mercy of Parliament.

Following news of the Boston Tea Party in reaction to unfair taxes in the North, another meeting in Rowan County sent ripple waves across the South. The freeholders (sole owners of a piece of land) sent delegates to a larger provincial convention. The future States of America began to be United as fellow rebels joined together.

Rowan County was among the first in the South to organize a Committee of Public Safety. This local committee included Morgan Bryan Jr. and Colonel Jonathan Hunt from Shallow Ford. More than a dozen resolutions were agreed to, most regarding unfair taxes, but two resolutions stand out: "That the cause of the town of Boston is the common cause of the American colonies" and "That the African slave trade is injurious to this colony." This language was born in a well-considered statement by responsible citizens. A local community in present Davidson County chose the name Lexington in solidarity with the Massachusetts town where blood had been shed.

Soon Samuel Bryan, the fist fighter and Patriot Morgan Bryan Jr.'s brother, became a lieutenant colonel of the British Royal Army with a company of local militiamen, no doubt crossing over Shallow Ford to gain access to the Salem to Cape Fear Road, to join with the larger forces. The Loyalists, however, were pursued and beaten decisively at Moore's Creek Bridge. Samuel Bryan was one of the few Tory officers to escape. This battle was significant because, first, it predated the signing of the Declaration of Independence by five months; second, fellow colonists fought one another; and finally, Patriots stopped Loyalists from reinforcing the British troops. After Moore's Creek, the British reanalyzed their strategy of relying on strong Loyalist support in the South and shifted their attention back to the North. This Patriot victory in the revolution counted among the defeated Samuel Bryan, the scion of Bryan's Settlement.

Samuel Bryan strove to make Bryan's Settlement a stronghold of Loyalists for the next year, while fighting skirmishes with roving bands of Patriots. This new version of Eden was troubled. Morgan Bryan's sons became known as Loyalists.

The youngest son, Thomas Bryan, an ensign in the Tory militia, became the first known casualty of the Whig-Tory struggle in the area when, in 1776, he was beaten and killed by a Whig ferryman while crossing the Yadkin River. He may have died very near the place where, as a ten-year-old boy, he had arrived in his new homeland. He left a widow, Sarah, daughter of Jonathan Hunt, and children; years later, Sarah would marry widower and preacher John Gano.

Other Bryans fled the escalating conflict between family and neighbors. Fortunately, they had a place to go where family members had already blazed a trail. Bryan brothers Morgan Jr., James and William (married to Daniel Boone's sister Mary) made multiple trips to Kentucky to clear land, plant crops and build temporary dwellings in the new Bryan Settlement there, the chosen frontier of their generation. But escaping the war was not easy. Ironically, they were perceived as Tories by association in Kentucky, and some returned home; it was never a simple choice, laced with tragedy.

James Bryan's wife died, and Rebecca Boone cared for their six children along with her own; William and his son were killed on the frontier of Kentucky by Indians, just like brother-in-law William Linville and his son were. Daniel and Rebecca Boone also suffered the deaths of two of their sons. The dilemma in this human migration came down to deciding which risk to take. At the end of the century, only one of the seven sons of Morgan Bryan, John Bryan and his family, had remained in the Shallow Ford area, and with his death in 1800, the Bryan Settlement on the Yadkin River dwindled significantly, a half century after being the first there.

One area of repeated occupation, if not military conflict, by troops during the revolution was the Moravian settlement of Wachovia. The Moravians were not pacifists (as commonly thought), but they were neutral in the War for Independence. They were here as guests of the British government but felt called to be hospitable, even to their enemies, making them easy marks for troops needing food and suspicious to both sides. Remaining neutral, even as they sympathized with their neighbors, would prove impossible, and they paid a high price.

The Moravians noted on May 13, 1775, that a storm left hail three feet deep "over a strip fourteen miles long and four wide, and was accompanied by a flood which ruined several plantations" in the vicinity of Shallow Ford;

Joseph Bryan came to Salem for supplies and spoke of how damaged his plantation was. The natural fears of flooding, always a constant along rivers, were overshadowed by the war looming on the horizon.

The month before the Revolutionary War came to the Shallow Ford area, on September 9, 1780, the commander of the southern theater of the war, Patriot Major General Horatio Gates, wrote to Virginia governor Thomas Jefferson about the situation in the South following the Patriots' defeat at Camden. The Papers of Thomas Jefferson relate Gates's assessment of important strongholds when he penned, "Should Wilmington in this state or Portsmo[uth] in Yours, be the posts they intend to take, I conceive the Southern Army would be intirely misplaced at Charlotte, Salisbury and the Ford upon the Yadkin." Gates was mistaken and would be replaced, but he particularly underestimated the importance of the ford on the Yadkin or that it would be up to Continental army soldiers to hold it. Local Patriots would defend the Shallow Ford on the Yadkin. Soon it became an important stage of revolutionary history.

By the fall of 1780, the war had come in earnest to the Shallow Ford area, though mostly still fought between neighbors. Few fighters wore British uniforms, an indicator that it was mostly Carolinians fighting one another. Yadkin historian Lewis Shore Brumfield stated, "For the first years of the Revolution, Shallow Ford escaped military action, but being such a strategic place this luck could not hold out." It was just a matter of time, and that time was 1780. In less than an hour, the place became known as Battle Branch.

A week after the Patriots were victorious over the Loyalists at the Battle of Kings Mountain, the winners were on the move—some militiamen returning home for harvest season, and others were transporting the hundreds of Loyalists taken prisoner. Also, Whig colonel Martin Armstrong of Surry County communicated with Jethro Sumner that "the men I have cannot be depended on & of a truth my present Circumstances are bad" and "unless some timely aid comes am afraid the enemy will persevere further in their hostile Scheme already begun," according to the *Colonial and State Records of North Carolina*.

Moravian records stated on October 12, 1780, "A company of Whigs had to be fed here. They went on toward the Shallow Ford and…met a strong company of Tories. The Whigs refused to surrender and there was a hand-to-hand fight, in which the Tories killed one or two, and took several prisoners. Many of the Tories came here during the night to get bread to eat, but were very mannerly; they were in this neighborhood to see after the Whigs." The next morning, the record continued: "[S]ixteen horsemen arrived; they were very wild and threatened that this town would be burned to the ground within a few days." Skirmishes increased as tension around Shallow Ford intensified.

Early on the morning of October 14, the inevitable happened. About 150 Patriots from Surry and Rowan Counties began patrolling in search of Tories. A group of more than 100 militiamen from Montgomery County, Virginia, under the leadership of Major Joseph Cloyd had arrived the night before and almost doubled the number of locals waiting in the woods. Shortly after 9:00 a.m. on that autumn morning, the peace at Shallow Ford was disturbed when the North Carolina and Virginia Patriots joined ranks. When the Tories crossed the ford, the fight that had been building for weeks finally happened in the Battle of Shallow Ford.

The Tories crossing Shallow Ford were led by brothers Gideon and Hezekiah Wright of Surry County and Captain James Bryan of Rowan County. The Wright brothers were veterans of the French and Indian War and had sided with British governor Tryon in the Regulators War.

James Bryan had gone to Kentucky with family but returned a few days before with his father, Morgan Bryan Jr. They separated upon arrival, as his father supported the Patriot cause and James was a Loyalist. This war was not just brother against brother, but also father against son.

On Mulberry Fields Road, the combined Patriots, believed to be 350 to 400 men from North Carolina and Virginia, encountered the band of Tories (estimates range between 400 and 900) coming from the direction of the river, having just crossed Shallow Ford. With the Patriots waiting for the enemy, they encountered each other and quickly fell into battle mode in the cover of the trees. Whichever side fired first, the others joined in.

The place in the woods where the two sides collided appears very much today as it did then. The ground would have been covered with fallen and slippery leaves, with enough leaves left clinging to the trees to provide some cover to hide the darting soldiers. Accounts indicate that the ground may have also been wet with a heavy dew.

Intense fighting ensued for about forty-five minutes. One can imagine buckskin-clad men with muskets dashing from tree to tree accompanied by the noise of fallen leaves crunching beneath their feet and impromptu commands being yelled. It is likely many of them personally knew those on the other side and that they called out to them by name, confounding an already confusing scenario. The sounds of horses trampling and shouts and ammunition rippled through the trees and probably ricocheted, creating a maze of death. Darting from tree to tree to try to gain an advantage even while shielding themselves, the furtive movements in no way resembled the traditional British military style of fighting. This was backwoods fighting, an organic survival mode born of necessity on the frontier.

The first to fall was probably the Whig commander, Captain Henry Francis, one of the Virginians who arrived the night before. Francis was fighting alongside his two sons, Henry Jr. and John, who in turn killed the man who shot his father. Another Whig captain, Isaac Campbell, reckoned with his fear and fled. Captain James Bryan, who grew up down the road, was killed. Tory John Pace and at least one of his sons were among the dead buried in an unmarked mass grave. When it was over, fifteen Tories had been killed and three wounded were taken prisoner; three Whigs were wounded. The Whigs buried Captain Francis astride the Mulberry Fields Road, where today a modern tombstone marks the final resting place of a Virginian who died defending North Carolina soil.

Andrew Carson stated in his war pension application that with no higher-ranking officer, the Whig captains commanded their own men. Captain Carson himself had ridden through the night to William Lee Davidson, asked and was given fifty-two men to help the Whigs defend Shallow Ford.

Topography alongside the river played a crucial role in the outcome. The Patriots pushed their advantage of occupation in the grove of trees as the Tories, after taking a stand initially, were forced to retreat backward between trees, first uphill at the site of the most intense engagement and then downhill as they moved back toward the Shallow Ford, all the time with more of their own troops behind them crossing the river and pushing into them. The retreating Tories were running into their own men. It was chaos.

The surviving Tories ran back toward Shallow Ford to escape across the river. George Kimbrough (reportedly an enslaved man but unconfirmed), fishing on the river that morning, recalled hearing the Tories yell, "We are whipped! We are whipped!" to their fellow soldiers coming toward them. Normally a quiet fishing spot, Shallow Ford was anything but that morning.

Events played out as only they could have. The water splashed as horses were reined in, running into one another, stumbling and falling, no doubt throwing their panicky riders while others on foot struggled for sure footing, running on slippery rocks and avoiding the flailing horses as best they could. Yells filled the air as the water and soil alike were churned up in a hasty retreat.

One lone Black Loyalist named Ball Turner was separated from his troop and continued to fire until taken down. From beginning to end, the whole battle lasted less than an hour, although it no doubt felt like an eternity to those in the woods that fateful morning.

Patriot Colonel Joseph Williams had heard that the enemy was approaching. He rode in toward the conclusion of the fight and saved a wounded Tory from retribution at the butt of a gun in the hands of a Patriot. Colonel Williams, from his nearby Panther Creek home, no doubt knew personally and had interacted many times with the Wright brothers and other Tories.

Then Colonel John Peasley rode in with three hundred men from Salisbury. They quickened their pace when they heard the sound of musket fire. In a report, he wrote, "Last Saturday, we were within almost one and a half miles of the Shallow Ford when we heard a foray. Thinking that our light infantry was engaged, we advanced with all possible speed and discovered that the Virginians and some of the Surry troops had attacked three hundred Tories under Colonel Wright." When they realized how the battle was falling out, there were distant cries of "Victory for Liberty! Huzzah! Huzzah!" from the Salisbury men, according to Galloway Reynolds.

The Battle of Shallow Ford was an important turning point, much more than a chance encounter and skirmish. The Tories may have seemed to be advancing but the Patriots had them exactly where they wanted: trapped between a hard place and a river. While most of the Tories escaped, they dispersed and disbanded, never to reorganize with quite the same force.

Remarkably, this battle was fought between local militias with the help of the Virginians. As no Continental or British troops were involved, no formal reports were filed—the Whigs had no single leader and the Tories retreated and scattered. But that last result was the key ingredient in this significant victory. The added resistance the Wright brothers' troops could have provided Cornwallis was lost and never regained.

In the two centuries since, hardwoods and pines grew strong and tall as their roots reached to a branch of the Yadkin, formerly called Bucking Branch but after 1780 known as Battle Branch, as the water flowed red with the blood of the dead and wounded. One strong, silent witness still stands as a natural monument to the bravery and sacrifice in this special place. The Big Poplar Tree is a single massive giant that rises above the surrounding trees, its top oddly misshapen (legends say the result of an encounter between Greene and Cornwallis in the tree's youth, but since

Big Poplar Tree at Battle Branch. *Courtesy of author.*

they were never there at the same time, it was more likely trampled by men or horses in this battle). Its trunk is so large now that it takes seven adults holding hands with outstretched arms to encircle it. It remains as the lone surviving witness of the Battle of Shallow Ford.

The Patriots arrived throughout the night at Bethabara demanding food. Upward of four hundred men descended, requiring cattle be killed, bread be baked and all the stores of milk and butter be emptied. The Moravians, taken advantage of by both sides, wrote that the Patriots "forced their way into our houses and seized all stores in the town" and "behaved badly." Moravians may not have had a dog in this fight, but if they had, it would have been taken.

In the next few days, the Moravians wrote that "the woods were full of Liberty men on horseback, looking for Tories." Patriots continued to show up as word spread quickly that the enemy had been beaten, roaming the woods in hopes of flushing out more targets but mostly celebrating. Morale was boosted across the South by the news of the Tories being turned away from entering the Forks of the Yadkin at Shallow Ford.

On October 19, only five days after the Battle of Shallow Ford, the state Board of War sent a message to the North Carolina Assembly delegates that read, "Inclosed you have the account of Lord Cornwallis's Retreat from Charlotte with precipitation, by reason, as we suppose, of Ferguson's Defeat; as also the killing and dispersing a Number of Tories at the Shallow Ford….These events are truely interesting to this State, and give a Sprightly Countenance to our affairs, so lately clouded and embarrassed." The numbers of Tories killed or captured at Kings Mountain and those dispersed at Shallow Ford tipped the scales in favor of the Patriots. One year to the day before Cornwallis would surrender to George Washington at Yorktown, the State of North Carolina acknowledged Shallow Ford's role in turning the course of the campaign. From that point on, the Patriots would have the advantage, just as they had in the woods of Battle Branch.

Also on October 19, a field council was held by Patriots on the nearby farm of Abraham Creson. In that meeting, Colonel Armstrong, along with Colonel Williams and nine other officers, issued an offer to Loyalists involved that if they came to the county seat of Richmond by November 1 and turned in their horses, weapons and ammunition, Williams would use his influence with the state assembly to gain a pardon for them. Not many a man living in colonial North Carolina would surrender his horse or his guns.

Colonel Joseph Williams owned the Panther Creek plantation located the east side of the river in a community known as "Little Yadkin." He and his wife, Rebekah, had thirteen children, including eight sons (four of whom she later bravely rescued from Cornwallis's wrath), most of whom served in public office. His sons became clerks of court and state adjutant general, and Lewis Williams was for nearly three decades a representative in the U.S. House of Representatives, known as the "Father of the House." Several children of the patriarch migrated to Tennessee, including among their descendants one of the first U.S. senators to represent the new state and a twentieth-century playwright, Tennessee Williams.

Meanwhile, the Patriots were marching the prisoners from Kings Mountain toward the crossing at Shallow Ford. More than six hundred Tories had been taken prisoner—not British troops but regional Loyalists. A few were executed, but many more escaped, through the woods or even hiding under the water at a river crossing. After a while, the Patriots lost heart for killing or pursuing their fellow Carolinians, and as they were running low on food, the immediate goal became finding food and a real army to take the prisoners. The number of participants in the march diminished as Patriots headed back home when a convenient road presented itself. They crossed Shallow Ford ten days after the conflict at Battle Branch.

The prisoner march was commanded by Major Joseph Winston of Surry County; the budding business town next to Salem would be later named for him. Some Loyalist prisoners saw the wisdom of switching sides. Of the 600 original prisoners in the march to prison, fewer than 130 eventually made it to Hillsborough. On October 23, the Moravians recorded an eclipse of the sun—they hoped that it was a sign of better days to come. Then General Cornwallis entered the war in the South.

Lieutenant General Charles, Earl Cornwallis, was a fascinating individual. As eldest son, he inherited land, titles and a seat in the House of Lords in Parliament. However, he chose to live his life in the military, something normally younger sons without an inheritance did. He spent much of his adult life fighting on foreign soil and died doing so in India. Cornwallis is an intriguing study in contrasts. Highly educated and endowed, he fought a fight not his own. Before he ever led the British forces to fight the American colonists, he had been among a group of five lords who voted in Parliament to not saddle the colonies with the oppressive taxes and even expressed sympathy and support for the colonists.

In spite of his lengthy military absences, he was a good family man, with all indications of having a loving marriage (not always the case among the British aristocracy) with his wife, Jemima. He left the war in New York, where he repeatedly chased George Washington, to return home to tend to his ill wife, who died young in 1779.

When Cornwallis returned after his wife's death, he was reassigned to the struggle in the South. Perhaps his sympathy for the colonists and his tender grief played a role in a departure from his reputation as a great military strategist; several times he failed to pursue the Patriots in the Carolinas when he could have. While he was the enemy, he may have been the most generous enemy the Patriots could have had. Numerous times when troops wanted to torch and destroy property, he would not allow it.

Charles Cornwallis began his southern command in South Carolina. He strove to occupy North Carolina, as it was a sanctuary for hotheads and staging ground for control of the South. That would not prove to be easy. He did not find the concentrated numbers of Loyalists he had been led to believe would rally behind him. Many local sympathizers had become alienated. Upon encountering the scrappy North Carolinians in Charlotte, he described them as a "veritable hornet's nest of rebellion." Cornwallis uttered an insult that the twentieth-century Charlotte Hornets basketball team would proudly take for their mascot.

Nathanael Greene was the commander of the Patriots against whom General Cornwallis would race across North Carolina. Greene was not a southerner, but he became one after the war, and his name is honored in the two cities of Greenville in both Carolinas and Greensboro, as well as in seventeen other states.

Greene was not as likely a military leader as his foe. He was born into a Quaker pacifist family in Rhode Island, and a childhood limp prevented him being an officer of the local militia he organized. He proved valuable to General George Washington in the Continental army as a scrappy tactician, and they became great personal friends. George Washington and Nathanael Greene were the only two American generals to serve in the Continental army from the first skirmishes in Boston until the British surrendered in 1783. Had Greene not thwarted Cornwallis in the South and the British won, he and Washington could have been tried for treason in London.

Nathanael Greene also had a love match in marriage to Catharine and fathered seven children during his decade-long military career. After the war, he accepted one of many plantations offered him as a hero in the South and farmed in Georgia. He died there of sunstroke at only forty-three years old and in debt, having supplied his troops with personal loans.

Greene's widow, Caty, continued to live at their Georgia plantation, where she rented a room to a young scientist name Eli Whitney. Legend persists that she played a small role in the invention of the cotton gin, which would revolutionize the production of cotton and the South's economy. In one last chapter of ties born during battle days, shortly after Caty died in 1814, a disheveled castaway came ashore to the family plantation on Cumberland Island—the once gallant Henry "Light-Horse Harry" Lee had fallen on hard times, and a few weeks later he died in the home of his good friend Nathanael Greene's daughter on the South Carolina coast. His son Robert E. Lee was eleven years old.

Back in 1778, Nathanael Greene was handpicked by General George Washington to replace the most recent of a string of commanders in the South. That Washington would sacrifice this man demonstrates not only a vote of confidence in Greene but also how much Washington valued a decisive victory in the South. Greene knew that it was an impossible task and could doom his military career. He went anyway.

The American army was in terrible disarray in the southern colonies. The men were disorganized, underfed and badly outfitted, and random victories were not followed up. Furthermore, the British army had strengthened its position by sending General Cornwallis with fresh troops to rally Loyalists, secure Georgia with its important harbor of Savannah and sweep through the Carolinas and into Virginia toward victory. Nathanael Greene and Charles Cornwallis had not yet met and would not for a while longer.

Major General Nathanael Greene learned of Kings Mountain on his way south to the southern resistance. The Battle of Kings Mountain was a dramatic Patriot victory when British major Patrick Ferguson trapped himself on a hill, hoping in vain that Cornwallis would come to his rescue. He found himself surrounded on a hilltop with no escape route except to fight his way down the hill. Remarkably, he had time to write a letter to a former teacher while under siege that read, "Between you and I, there has been an inundation of Barbarians, rather larger than expected."

Ferguson soon met a barbaric band of nine hundred outlanders (who had been encouraged by a stirring Presbyterian sermon on Gideon the night before) when the Overmountain Men came charging down the mountains. These mountain dwellers had no problem climbing a hill after first putting a piece of white paper in their hats (since neither side was in uniform and they did not want to shoot their compatriots—the Loyalists stuck in pine sprigs). Not only were they ferocious, but since they lived on land illegally, they also stood to lose everything if the British won.

Ferguson bravely led a bayonet charge, where he was killed along with 320 of his men; the captured were marched to the Moravian town of Salem, where a British doctor treated Whig and Tory alike. In the Battle of Kings Mountain, Ferguson was the only regular soldier and only British citizen involved; it was a conflict between American neighbors.

Arriving in Charlotte, Nathanael Greene found a scattered, forlorn remnant of Patriot troops. But he did have a burly relative of his friend

George named William Washington and the legendary Virginian Daniel Morgan. Greene began a nightly writing campaign on a portable desk in his tent to recruit troops and supplies for reinforcement. Perhaps his most valuable contribution was this power of the pen over the sword. A British commander said of Greene that he was "indefatigable in collecting troops and leading them to be defeated" but that "the more he is beaten, the farther he advances in the end."

General Greene had to whip southern Patriots into fighting shape. He recruited a young law student in Salisbury by the name of William Richardson Davie to be the army's commissary. Davie was British born but had proven himself as a cavalry commander. They worked to clothe the troops, hiring women to sew for them and paying them in valuable salt (like the Romans, who gave the term *salary* from the Latin word for salt). Greene initiated a prisoner exchange proposal with Cornwallis and commissioned a prisoner of war camp to be built in the town of Salisbury.

One of Greene's first ideas was to investigate how to make the Yadkin River navigable from Charleston. He proposed building flatboats that would balance the weight of heavy transports. He may have been the first to suggest making the Yadkin River accessible from the ocean, but he would not be the last.

Greene wrote in letters of the abundance of rivers and creeks but noted that they were a barrier. He would use this to his advantage. His master plan of trapping Cornwallis on the opposite side of these rivers was born of necessity. It worked. At one point, when Greene was keeping Cornwallis trapped on the other side of the Catawba River, the importance of this geographical strategy was clear. As John S. Pancake stated, "[O]utside of Green's tent, the rain stopped. It was if an alarm bell had sounded. In a matter of hours, the floodwaters would drop and the fords would be passable for the pursuing enemy. It was time to move." Another time, the roar of floodwaters hid the sounds of the British approaching. The weather and the flooding rivers called the shots in this fight.

Daniel Morgan and Colonel Washington's cavalry won the Battle of Cowpens in South Carolina. The Patriots also confiscated wagons of supplies, a mobile forge and even the buglers with their instruments. The British retreated, torching their supplies along the way in the pouring cold rains, which turned the roads into muddy trenches and the rivers into gushing rapids.

Then Greene defied all military logic and divided his troops, with about six hundred men going with Daniel Morgan up into the backcountry.

Greene took the remainder and headed east. Being greatly outnumbered by the British troops, such a maneuver would surely make either portion vulnerable, but he guessed that Cornwallis would not divide to conquer. He guessed correctly.

The Race to the Dan River in Virginia ensued. This campaign would bring General Cornwallis to Shallow Ford. The immediate goal for Greene was to keep Cornwallis from reaching Virginia, where supplies and reinforcements waited for him along with a clear path north. Traitor Benedict Arnold had a British stronghold in Portsmouth. On the other side, General Washington had sent Lafayette to help Greene along the Virginia border. The Race to the Dan was about who would get there first and win the prize of famous assistance.

Greene, knowing that he would always be outnumbered, strategized to always be ahead of Cornwallis and, even when beaten, inflict unrecoverable damages. Greene never won a military conflict outright against the British but is credited with victory in that he persistently wore down Cornwallis's troops until they could no longer fight.

Since controlling the river fords was crucial, Greene left five hundred men to guard the ford on the Catawba River and then moved his troops. Cornwallis faked a crossing at another ford but was foiled by a guard who fled and caused them to cross at the wrong place. In the end, it did not go well for either army. The river pulsated with dead and wounded British soldiers and their horses; William Lee Davidson of the Patriots was killed. With their leader down, the troops fled back toward Salisbury, colliding with astonished civilians fleeing the sounds of battle with some Brits in pursuit. They all converged at Tarrants Tavern, where confusion reigned. Greene, who had been waiting for troops in Salisbury, sent out word that the meeting place had changed to Guilford Courthouse, and the die was cast.

While in Salisbury, General Greene met Mrs. Steele, the mistress of the tavern. According to Rowan history, when she heard him say that he was "tired, hungry, alone and penniless," she gave him all her savings in the form of two small bags of coins. Greene removed a picture of King George III from the wall, wrote on the back the words "O George, hide thy face and mourn" (or "blush," some said) and rehung it, facing the wall. Supposedly, the picture hung in that way for many years as testament to Salisbury's loyalty and the generosity of one woman.

Cornwallis chased Greene, whose local subordinates knew the lay of the land (at one point, Cornwallis marched his troops in exactly the wrong direction). At Trading Ford, Generals Morgan and Greene found the Yadkin impassable on foot but commandeered all the boats, got to the other side and watched the water rise overnight.

The British troops arrived in Salisbury the next day. Legend says that one of the cavalry commanders charged his way through the Old Stone House still standing, but the steps are much too steep for a horse to mount; besides, he could have easily ridden around the house. British officer Charles O'Hare's reference to the area as the "end of the world" and its residents as "savages" are more reliable historically.

Cornwallis reached the impassable Yadkin River and could do nothing other than cannonade the American troops on the other side. Greene's command post, a small wooden cabin, shook, and the roof boards were shot off under the barrage of fire Cornwallis threw at them, all while Greene continued to write messages. Only the raging river separated one army from the other at this point. Engagement would have to wait until another day when they could be on the same side of the river.

Cornwallis, held up in Salisbury, wrote, "I am distressed by the rivers and creeks being swelled, but shall try to pass the Yadkin at the shallow ford as soon as possible." Having cut himself off from his supply chain, Cornwallis delayed to have his men slaughter some cattle. Colonel Francis Locke of the local militia partially destroyed a small bridge that British scouts were attempting to cross, requiring time to repair it. Cornwallis was delayed by cows, bridges and rivers in his race.

The weather was, by all accounts, wretched in January 1781. Rains were called a "deluge" and often in the form of ice and snow. The dilemma that winter weather hands southerners still, that of melting during the day and refreezing overnight, created a frustrating scenario.

Then Cornwallis discovered buck tallow. When it got wet, it became slippery and walking in it was like trudging through slime. Supply wagons were burned because heavily laden wagon wheels simply could not roll through this dense clay. Cornwallis famously said it was like trudging through "pudding" (think British figgy, not soft ones), and the name of Pudding Ridge near Farmington stuck like the mud. Add ice and the surfaces were even more dangerous, hard on horseshoes and shoe leather alike. When the British had destroyed their supplies, the men were allowed to carry extra soles they had confiscated at Ramsour's Mill.

Both sides moved troops during the night because if the ground was frozen, it was easier for man and horse to get their footing than in the melted slush of the day. Veterans told of their shoes and feet being ripped to shreds by unseen rocks in the icy mud. Roads that were ordinarily bad became treacherous trenches, impassable to wagons. Low areas turned into swamps. Marching at night, it was senseless to make camp; quick cold food and naps against trees became the routine.

Cornwallis's trek to Shallow Ford from Trading Ford had to be accomplished cross-country, not following the river, as some speculated. There was not a road along the river for one thing and he needed to accumulate supplies and food. Cornwallis looked to take the simplest route. The distance between Trading Ford and Shallow Ford is twenty-four miles as the crow flies, but it is believed to be more like forty miles by the roads that existed then, awful as they were.

There is debate still about the exact route Cornwallis took across the land in present Davie County between the two fords. He was in a hurry in this race, as much as an army can be. He had to rely on scouts and locals pointing the way, and he had to cross a lesser body of water called Dutchmans Creek.

Unbeknownst to Cornwallis, Dutchmans Creek had recently played a significant role in life of Daniel Boone. A half century later, when Boone researcher Lyman Draper interviewed Daniel's youngest child, Nathan, after his father died, Nathan Boone responded to queries of what his legendary father had told him about his home in Davie County, with his first statement being, "I remember the name Dutchmans Creek." Daniel and Rebecca had lived the longest spell early in their marriage in a cabin on the Sugar Tree Creek, which fed into the creek, and Daniel had hunted along Cornwallis's next obstacle.

Exactly where Cornwallis crossed Dutchmans Creek between the town of Mocksville and Pudding Ridge is uncertain. A creek might seem to be an easy crossing compared to the river ahead, but creeks pose their own challenges. Dutchmans Creek is a coursing body of water that, over centuries, carved its channel deeply within the hard buck tallow clay. Deep-water channels can be difficult for horses and impossible for wagons to cross. The challenge was to cross Dutchmans Creek at a critical place where the banks were low enough, preferably where a working road already existed. Many local historians believe that this road may have been the current Highway 158 that then led east from present-day Mocksville toward Salem. Just before the old Farmington Road origins on Highway 158, a small bridge takes modern traffic across Dutchmans Creek at a low spot that no doubt has existed from early walking paths. There was an early mill east of today's bridge, Brown's, whose building was relocated later into Mocksville and served as J.C. Green Milling Company; a mill also required low, flat access to the creek and accessibility for customers.

Brown's Mill on Dutchmans Creek. *Martin-Wall History Room.*

The logical conclusion is that Cornwallis loosely followed the modern roads of Highway 601 from Salisbury to Mocksville and then headed east along present Highway 158, crossing Dutchmans Creek where the bridge still does and then veering north along current Farmington Road to get to Shallow Ford. This would have taken him through the Pudding Ridge and Farmington area.

It is unlikely that Greene and Cornwallis ever saw each other during the Race to the Dan. Greene was east of the Yadkin River, moving away as fast as he could when Cornwallis arrived at Shallow Ford. Cornwallis had to wait several days, like so many others in history, for the waters to recede to a safe level; it gave Greene time to maneuver.

Cornwallis and his army crossed the Yadkin at Shallow Ford on February 8, 1781, when Jethro Rumple wrote of a young John Spurgen spotting them and getting a message to Greene of their whereabouts. The crossing of the Yadkin River by a large troop and their animals and minimal supply train was not quick or secretive. This was a proper army on the march, no doubt one of the days Shallow Ford saw its greatest concentration of traffic. No one captured the image of this huge influx of armed humanity and horseflesh, but its significance as the only way Cornwallis could continue the Race to the Dan created a moment in time when the watery path across the river played a major role in much larger events. Shallow Ford was the eye of the needle for Cornwallis.

Rebekah Williams, wife of Colonel Joseph Williams, was at home on the Panther Creek plantation with four children, her husband absent fighting in the war, when word reached her of Cornwallis's approach. According to the story in the Williams family genealogy, she and a slave slipped away to hide in the woods with her small boys, the youngest one Nathaniel only two weeks old. After hiding in the cold a long time, they returned to find the house and all their stores of food raided. Nathaniel caught a cold that day in the woods and was always sickly until his young death.

The British troops then made their way to Salem. Along the way, they pillaged a farm, where they took all the farmwife's grain, corn, meat and chickens, according to Francis Ketner's pension application. They demanded to know where her husband was; her retort was that "he was gone with a wagon to haul a load of ammunition to the American army to shoot you redcoats that have robbed me and my living." In Salem, Cornwallis's men stole the long johns of the single brethren off their clothesline. Nothing and no one was safe.

Meanwhile, Greene met Daniel Morgan and Henry "Light-Horse Harry" Lee and made a plan. Having made Cornwallis race across the Piedmont and deplete his supply line, Greene knew that they had to meet ultimately and chose the place to be Guilford Courthouse. He pushed forward to reach the Dan River and obtain reinforcements first. As Greene biographer Elswyth Thane put it, "Geography and the weather were now to become the dominant factors in the long cat-and-mouse game of strategic retreat that would make Greene famous."

Greene reached the Dan River with the British troops chasing him. Alongside another river, for three cold, wet and miserable days, the two armies paralleled each other. "Light-Horse Harry" Lee guarded the rear of the Americans just ahead of Cornwallis on the west. At one point, Lee led his enemy on a pursuit of him, hid in the woods as they passed and then harassed the rear of their troops. After Greene won the Race to the Dan and got what he needed, Cornwallis headed back to recruit more Loyalists. Greene's army made his way to the place where he had determined to do battle, Guilford Courthouse.

Greene meticulously described why he steered Cornwallis toward that place: it was the perfect battle site, with open fields behind fences and woods on the sides—ideal for cover and retreat as needed. Cornwallis had to be the aggressor in order to claim the land and deliver a victory to London. Greene and his men only had to hold on.

The opposing armies finally met on March 15. Lee kept journals and gave the most comprehensive and colorful account of that day's conflict in his memoirs (which his son Robert E. Lee would transcribe into publication years later). In the standard eighteenth-century European military style, the battleground was set up like a choreographed play, with both sides lined up shoulder to shoulder and waiting for cues. (British historian Angus Konstam described the Carolinian militiamen in a typical British understatement as being "less reliable" in this orchestrated battle style.)

Greene ordered each line of militiamen to fire two volleys and then fall back to make room for the next. Then cavalries charged in with bugles blaring, and the battle commenced. The hand-to-hand combat between the trained British and the stubborn Americans appeared at first to be going in favor of stubbornness.

Charles Cornwallis—exhausted, frustrated and in desperate need of a victory—changed the course of the battle in one drastic, dramatic decision. He ordered his artillery to fire grapeshot from their cannons at close range into where both friend and foe were engaged in hand-to-hand combat. Even Cornwallis's own commanders were aghast that redcoats were being slaughtered along with the Patriots. General Greene, stunned to see Cornwallis cannonade the melee time after time, ordered a retreat to save lives. The battle lasted less than two hours. The British losses amounted to 27 percent, heavy on officers, whereas the American casualties were only 6 percent. British officer Charles O'Hare wrote, "I wish it had produced one substantial benefit to Great Britain, on the contrary, we feel at the moment the sad and fatal effects our loss on that day, nearly one half of our best Officers and Soldiers were either killed or wounded, and what remains are so completely worn out by the excessive Fatigues of the campaign, in a march of above a thousand miles, most of them barefoot…has totally destroyed this army." Believing that Cornwallis would capitalize on his victory, Greene had his men prepare fortifications overnight for the next attack that never came.

The remnants of Cornwallis's troops limped back in cold rain (as always, it seemed) toward Wilmington the following day, leaving behind the land they had fought for unclaimed and their wounded in the Americans' care, behind a white flag. The British had won the battle by killing their own. It was not a spectacular victory. Charles James Fox of the British Parliament summed it up: "Another such victory would ruin the British Army." General Cornwallis would not conquer the Carolinas and occupy Virginia. The South now belonged to the rabblerousing Americans, whose troops were led by a bookish, lame, letter-writing Quaker from Rhode Island. Rarely would the South owe so much to a northerner.

The Battle of Guilford Courthouse was the turning point in the War for Independence in the South. While technically won by the British, their losses made them unable to capitalize on the victory. Greene wrote, "They have met a defeat in a victory."

Shallow Ford played a role as one of many dominoes that had to fall at the right time in the right place. A shift of different direction at several points in the campaign could have changed the outcome at Guilford Courthouse, but the challenge of being able to get there had been foremost. The expression "the turning of the tide" aptly identifies the importance of the flooding of the Trading Ford and the accessibility at Shallow Ford. Cornwallis's crossing at Shallow Ford slowed him down, making it a pivotal point in a chain of events that allowed the beginning of the end of the War for Independence and, hence, the creation of the new nation of the United States.

The tide had indeed turned. Cornwallis retreated to Wilmington and, with his remaining British troops, skirted the coast to reach the eastern shore of Virginia. There he began building a fort at Yorktown, where he was eventually trapped and surrendered to Washington (although Cornwallis did not attend the official surrender and soon left for England, sailing with Benedict Arnold, a man in need of a new country) on October 19, just seven months after Guilford Courthouse. Konstam wrote that the majority of the troops Cornwallis surrendered had fought at Guilford Courthouse. He stated that Guilford proved to be the "first step on the road to a dramatic American victory, and to the independence of the United States of America." Church bells rang as the good news was rushed to southerners in towns along the old Great Wagon Road.

Colonel Samuel Bryan of Shallow Ford was captured and stood trial for treason in the Superior Court of Salisbury; it was argued that he had committed no crimes, other than take supplies for his men. Even William R. Davie, who had defeated him, spoke in support of Bryan. Nonetheless, Bryan and two other Tory leaders were convicted and sentenced to hang; they were imprisoned in the Salisbury prison (then on today's library front lawn), where its guards had to keep mobs from storming the prison to free him.

In the end, Samuel Bryan was pardoned in an act of reconciliation and civility and exchanged for Americans the British were holding, an elegant solution allowing the Americans to return home. His name appeared on a law authorizing the seizure of land owned by former Tories, but records do not reveal how much or if any land was taken. The Salisbury District Superior Court generously awarded nine hundred acres "where the family now lives." Bryan applied for compensation from the British for his service, but they refused. He had chosen the losing side and seen close relatives fall in the service of the lost cause. Bryan faced local censure and retreated to East Florida. Eventually, he came home to Bryan's Settlement and died on family land in 1798 after a tumultuous life. John K. Bryan wrote, "Given the deep interfamily hatreds generated during Rowan County's civil war, it is a tribute to the personal stature of Samuel Bryan that he could have returned to his land and lived out his life in peace among former enemies." It is also a tribute to his neighbors at Shallow Ford that offered him peace in the end.

Ironically, the final conflicts between the American Patriots and the British troops happened in the new western frontier and involved Daniel Boone from Dutchmans Creek. Boone described himself as a woodsman and no soldier or politician, yet he found himself being both by the end of the war he had tried to escape. Elected to represent the new settlements west of the mountains, he was in a meeting of the legislature in Richmond, standing out in his buckskin dress among colonials. Cornwallis was harassing the city, and some of his dragoons arrested Boone while he was attempting to save a number of horses. While imprisoned in a coal house, he sang, according to his son Nathan, like Paul and Silas in jail. He was released after agreeing to an oath to never take up arms again against the Crown, something he hoped to never do anyway.

Then Indian warriors led by British officers laid siege to Bryan's Station in Kentucky, a stockade where settlers fled for protection. Women and children bravely went for water outside the compound and kept them from dying of thirst. Daniel Boone brought his men from Boone's Station to rescue the fellow settlers and relatives. Boone let a "coward" remark get to him, and in a rare fit of anger he regretted the rest of his life, he rode across the river into an ambush leading other family members. Boone later related that it was one of the few times he killed an Indian outright in his life.

The Kentuckians had the advantage of better accuracy with their long rifles against the British muskets the Indians held. But the muskets could be reloaded quicker and in a volley of fire, followed by tomahawks and knives, the Indians fought back. Those with Boone retreated and he found himself abandoned. It was quickly over, and Daniel's son Israel, his eldest after the death of James, lay dead of a bullet shot to the heart. For the rest of his life, that day haunted Daniel Boone, the legend from Dutchmans Creek who thought he had escaped the war.

This Battle of Blue Licks was the last major battle of the War of Independence. The long war was over, the British having never regained control in the South after the Battle of Guilford Courthouse. Parliament in London decided to abandon any attempts to keep the American colonies and the peace treaty between what was now two nations was signed on September 3, 1783.

The vast majority of recorded Revolutionary War service by soldiers emerged when interviewed for government pensions, which was not approved and did not happen until 1832, fifty years after the war ended. Most soldiers who survived the war had died in the intervening years. The remainder had to rely on very old memories. Additionally, the Loyalists were seen as traitors and were reluctant to recount their activities. Many more recollections were lost over time, one of the handicaps of studying this period.

American Loyalists found themselves in a real spot of trouble, as they had chosen the losing side. British soldiers were imprisoned briefly, but they would all sail back across the pond. Loyalists were left living as traitors among the victors. Some lived with the shame, but many more, estimated at 100,000, fled for another part of the British empire—to Scotland or the British West Indies but mostly to Canada, where they were welcomed and given land grants for their service to the king. Canada became a little more American. Today, one-fifth of Canadians claim a Tory ancestor, as does this author, whose Canadian father was born in New Brunswick, where they settled barely over the border they had hastily crossed for safety. The Tories may not have won the war, but they did help populate Canada.

England would still control the largest empire in world history. The British empire reached its zenith following World War I, but the seeds of self-rule had been growing even as the empire did. The handing off of Hong Kong in 1997 marked the end of British colonial rule, but the end began with the American Revolution, which had its turning point at Shallow Ford.

One small community's story epitomizes the remarkable changes on the Yadkin River area during this time. About fifteen miles west of Shallow Ford was the colonial community of Houstonville, which grew up around a few families. Located in the eastern edge of present Iredell County, its name came from one of the early settlers, Christopher Houston. His story and that of Thomas Young and Andrew Carson tell what was both ordinary and extraordinary about the people of this area.

Thomas Young relocated from Virginia in 1778 to an area called Hunting Creek in then Rowan County. He was joined by neighbors Christopher Houston and Andrew Carson. They all had large families who intermarried and filled up the area.

Young sent three sons into the revolution, as well as three sons-in-law, including Andrew Carson and Major William Gill, who served as the aide to the commander-in-chief General Washington until the surrender at Yorktown. They both lived out their lives in Houstonville and are buried there.

Christopher Houston was a staunch Scot Presbyterian who defied the norms his entire life. He descended from Baron John Houston of Scotland, knighted on the battlefield of the Battle of Hastings for saving the life of the king. Christopher's father, Robert, smuggled grain from his farm into Valley Forge for Washington's troops. He was a distant cousin to the more famous Sam Houston.

Christopher migrated from Pennsylvania and met his future wife, Sarah, at Fort Dobbs when settlers retreated there for safety from Indian attacks. They settled on Hunting Creek and built the first mill there. He and his brother James signed on as captains with the North Carolina Rangers and fought together at the Battle of Ramsour's Mill, where James was killed. Christopher also assisted the Battle of Kings Mountain by holding at bay a group of Tories in the forks of the Yadkin River. Then, at Shallow Ford, he did the same. Finally, he fought in the Battle of Guilford Courthouse. Christopher recounted in later letters that he believed he lost most of his hearing during the war from sleeping on cold ground.

Houston founded the village that bore his name and was its first postmaster, as well as a justice of the peace and one of four men given the task of choosing a county seat—Statesville, so named to celebrate the new statehood. Then one of his children lured him to Tennessee. At the age of sixty-eight, Houston went over the mountains and started over. Unofficial records say that he owned 1,900 acres in present Iredell and Davie County and slaves, but he manumitted them in 1830 to the American Colonization Society, which transported them back to Africa and founded the country of Liberia.

Christopher Houston's son Placebo (an unusual family name) married Elizabeth Young and became the next postmaster of Houstonville, a post he held for many years in one of the earliest and longest lasting post offices in Iredell County. The Old Georgia Road passed very near it. Placebo also built a small log cabin that served as a school for his and neighboring children. At one time, the school's teacher was the mysterious Frenchman

Peter Stewart Ney, who not only taught farm boys to fence, play the flute and read French poetry but also claimed to have been Napoleon's fierce cavalry commander who escaped execution to live out his life in the backwoods. Placebo was also the recipient of lengthy letters written from his father, Christopher, in Tennessee (now in the holdings of Wilson Library at UNC) that provide the rich details of his military service, such as one noting "made havoc on Tory raids."

As well as being a soldier and pioneer repeatedly, Christopher Houston was a literate man with a library. Mentions of it showed up in his letters, where he wrote of spending one dollar for Whitefield's Sermons. He was well traveled and well read.

Andrew Carson typified the Scots-Irish who poured into the western foothills, but he was born here. His father, William Carson, had applied for an original Granville Land Grant but died of sunstroke working the land before the process could be completed. Andrew was described as a large man, a breeder of fine horses and somewhat impulsive but loyal, always answering the need to fight. His tombstone at the Houstonville cemetery states simply, "He was a soldier of the Revolutionary War." He repeatedly showed up when he heard of trouble, beginning with backcountry skirmishes, at Battle Branch with a troop of his own making and arriving the day after the Battle of Guilford Courthouse. Along the way, he married Temperance Young, became a farmer and recovered from several battle injuries. His brother Lindsay also fought in the war, most notably under General Wade Hampton.

In a great firsthand account, Andrew Carson's pension application told of one soldier's duty. He volunteered under the command of the famous Francis Marion, known as the Swamp Fox, delivering messages between Marion and Greene. He was remembered at the Battle of Camden as the "large Carolinian" who carried Baron de Kalb to dry land to die (a French volunteer—neither a baron nor a "de," but he was not the first to create a new identity upon migrating). Carson carried him after he was shot and bayonetted from the river; De Kalb did not survive and ended his storied life buried in a Camden churchyard, with his name given to many cities in the country for which he had died.

Carson then recounted multiple short tours of military service of days or weeks at a time when he showed up wherever there was action. Such was the nature of his participation as a voluntary ranger, always eager and most often arriving just in time.

In his pension application as a seventy-six-year-old man, fifty years after the war, Andrew Carson recalled:

> *Previous to the battle at Shallow Ford he was informed of the marching of the Tories and mounted his horse to ride 62 miles to Headquarters of General Davidson, where he arrived about sunrise next morning, who immediately gave him the command of 52 men, with which he returned and after maneuvering for two weeks he came upon and routed the main body of the Tories at Shallow Ford on the Yadkin after an obstinate engagement in which Captain Francis, a Whig was killed. There being no officer ranking above Captain—each one commanded his own men.*

A fascinating document held by the Iredell County Historical Society is a pass written on December 25, 1780, for this trio of men—Thomas Young, Christopher Houston and Andrew Carson—certified by a Rowan County justice of the peace. He had sworn from them that they were sending their wagons into Virginia for salt "to supply their distressed neighborhood." It further stated, "These are requesting all whom it may concern to let them pass and repass with their wagon and team, they having taken the oath of allegiance to their state and have taken an active part in the defense of the United States."

Lindsay Carson's military record is less well known, as he did not live long enough to file for a pension and quickly departed for the Kentucky frontier, where his family grew—his eldest son would marry into the Boone family. After his first wife died, he remarried Rebecca, and they produced ten more children, the last one born after his tragic death and named for him.

One more chapter to the Young-Houston-Carson family story in Houstonville was yet to unfold. Family legend and local letters tell the story that Lindsay and a pregnant Rebecca visited Andrew and Temperance Carson in Houstonville on December 24, 1809. A long-held tradition of a Christmas Eve celebration at the home of Christopher and Sarah Houston was a reunion of sort for the neighbors and visiting relatives. Rebecca went into labor. Sarah took her upstairs, and before long, the cries of a baby boy born on Christmas Eve in a place other than home added to the celebratory mood. Apparently out of gratitude to the host, the baby boy was named Christopher Houston Carson. History would know him as Kit.

While his birth was registered later in Madison County, Kentucky, and Kit himself stated that he was born there, local Iredell County residents have always claimed him, and with good evidence. First, Kit's words can be dismissed since he obviously would not remember the occasion. Second, his father was killed tragically by a tree falling when he was only nine years old and after his mother remarried a man Kit did not get along with, he ran away from home and never looked back, so his access to information was fleeting and perhaps flawed. An 1818 Christmas letter that Christopher Houston wrote mentioned having learned of Lindsay's death and expressed concern for only Kit by name, indicating a special relationship with that one child. Most convincing proof is the name itself. The fifteen children of Lindsay Carson were given only one name, mostly of biblical origins. Only one child stands out as unique: Christopher Houston Carson. Why else would he have been given this name? Houstonville may well have not only given some of its finest to the cause for American independence but also been the birthplace of the next trailblazer of the western frontier, Kit Carson.

CULTURAL REVOLUTION

Andy was only fourteen years old but life had already handed him heartache. His Scots-Irish parents, Andrew and Elizabeth Jackson, came from Ulster down the Great Wagon Road, perhaps crossing at Shallow Ford, and settled in the Waxhaw area in the Carolinas. Andy was born there (undetermined whether in present North or South Carolina), sadly three weeks after his father was killed in a logging accident while clearing his land. Andy never knew his father. Despite a difficult childhood, he was bright and, as a nine-year-old, often was given the job of reading the newspapers out loud to his mother's large family. It was their main source of information during the tumultuous revolution.

When the British slaughtered the Buford troops in Waxhaw, young Andy helped his mother tend to the wounded at Waxhaw Presbyterian Church. They fled when Cornwallis came to the Charlotte area. Andy and his brother Robert joined the local militia of Patriots and were captured. When ordered to clean the Tory officer's boots, Andy refused and was slashed by a sword. When ordered to lead them to a sympathizer's location, he took them the long way, allowing enough time for the target to escape. While confined to prison, his brother Robert contracted smallpox and died. Andy's mother went to Charleston, working as a nurse to support them financially, but then also died there.

At age fourteen, Andy was all alone in the world due to the hardships of pioneering and the cruelties of war. He learned law in Salisbury and jumped at the chance to go with a friend who was appointed a judge in the new western courts. He was in the first wagon train to use a new pass in the mountains that took him to Nashville. There he found his home for the rest of his life, except when he became the seventh president of the United States and the first one to be elected from the states west of the mountains. Historically, the "Age of Jackson" refers to a watershed era when political power was generated in the West, but Andrew Jackson was shaped by the forces in the Carolina Piedmont. He was a product of his time and those times, they were a-changin'.

This new republic, the United States of America, was a modern creation with no precedent. Not since Athens had a republic been intentionally designed. As a large-scale experiment, the new American nation experienced growing pains but also triumphs as it worked out the mechanics of a country governed of the people, by the people and for the people while the world watched and then followed its example. Out of 195 countries recognized by the United Nations in 2021, 159 countries claimed to have a republican form of government. In 1800, it was just one.

Huntsville was organized as a town in 1792 by Charles Hunt, son of pioneer Jonathan Hunt. While others of his generation fled west, he saw his fortune where he grew up. He bought 150 acres of land from the descendants of old Abraham Creson and ambitiously laid out plots for homes and businesses. The oldest extant house in Huntsville was built around 1800 on Lot 15 of the original town plot, where it still stands. Hunt also married well; his bride, Elizabeth Frohock, was related to a wealthy Salisbury clerk of court. The Hunts invested in Huntsville but lived in Salisbury, where records show that Charles Hunt was a prominent man, indicated by the fact that he was required to provide numerous buckets of water in case of a fire.

There had long been a blacksmith in Huntsville to meet the needs of travelers, but services quickly expanded. Doctors practiced medical care, and a common well in the town square provided water closer than the river. The Kelly Tavern offered lodging and meals for travelers and a post office for all.

Peter Clingman took over the family business, and the store (later called the Red Store) was greatly extended. He built a two-story building that provided housing for the storekeeper and family upstairs, a practical arrangement. Stores served so many purposes when still few and far between. Friends would meet and catch up on news. Known customers, in addition to buying staples they could not produce themselves, could get cash against a credit account, like a simple bank. Surviving ledgers offer intriguing insight into life, such as a July 1, 1823 entry that states, "Mrs. Mildred Kimbrough by

Circa 1800 log home in Huntsville. *Yadkin Public Library.*

George for 1 bottle of molasses, 18¾ [cents]." Offerings on the shelves of the store included everything from castor oil to silk handkerchiefs, saddle blankets and fishing hooks. Opium was even sold, for medicinal purposes, at one dollar per ounce. Records also reveal that Daniel Boone often stocked up on provisions there on his way toward the mountains, as did others who followed him to the Cumberland Gap. The place that continued to represent the frontier to those just arriving was now also the last touch with civilization for those departing.

Huntsville got a post office in 1795 due in part to its strategic location by the Shallow Ford (pioneers moving south would tell relatives to simply address their mail to Huntsville, knowing that they would hold it for them until claimed, a long-standing postal tradition). It was for a while the largest town west of the Yadkin River and was supposedly briefly considered for the state capital. By 1858, the Winston and Wilkesboro Plank Road had been built to run through Huntsville, and stagecoaches made regular stops. By the Civil War, the town had grown to a number of residents and stately houses, with a tavern, blacksmith, potter, two wagon makers, a millwright, doctor and the Red Store for supplies. The Ringling Brothers Circus came to town and pitched a tent. After Yadkin County was carved out of Surry in 1850 and the county seat of Yadkinville built, population and business shifted and Huntsville began to decline in population.

Huntsville was dealt a blow by Stoneman's Raid, which torched the store, but the blacksmith shop, which had repaired many a wagon wheel, operated until the 1950s. As of 2022, the public can get a good meal at Battle Branch Café and attend church in Huntsville.

As Lewis Brumfield Shore wrote, "The Shallow Ford area was the fruition of the ideas of the founding fathers, an agricultural society surrounding a village, where farmers, tradesmen and professional people all had their place, each with a valuable service to perform." A stable and thriving community in the early nineteenth century allowed people to live near Shallow Ford. It was no longer just a place in passing or a destination but a home for many.

Five miles east of Shallow Ford, the intersection of the Great Wagon Road and the road to Salem grew exponentially into the town of Lewisville, named for Lewis Laugenour. Earlier the place where pioneers on the Great Wagon Road rested before crossing to the new western frontier, it was incorporated into a town officially in 1991 in an extraordinary example of self-determination—the very element that had always quietly shaped its existence. About the same time, basketball star Chris Paul grew up in Lewisville, the descendant of pioneers himself—Peter Oliver, an early enslaved potter who earned his freedom in Salem, and Nathaniel Jones, the first Black owner of his own gas station in North Carolina, where Chris worked summers.

While the Shallow Ford remained very much the gateway to the Yadkin Valley, lesser roads became necessary as landlocked plots lay behind others. Once land was claimed, fences went up and fields were plowed. Much of the court litigation in the nineteenth century involved petitioning for public access across privately owned land. As early as 1758, the Rowan County court records list men responsible for the job of keeping up the roads. Road upkeep was assigned to the landowners; this meant more than just money, as they were required to list hands—how many able-bodied men, free or enslaved, they could supply when the road needed physical repair.

A county court granted requests for access or not, largely based on petitions by neighbors either way. Complaints in court literally stated how they could not petition the court if they could not get to the court.

One petition in 1839 marked the close of a chapter of history. In an intriguing November 1839 letter, oddly addressed to the Davie County justices as "The Worshipful County Court of Davie," the signers requested that they "humbly pray your worships that the Georgia Road crossing the Hunting Creek at Ward's Ford may be discontinued…as a public road and hereafter only kept as a public cartway. Among the reasons we offer…it is of but little use to the public no travelling passes it being so near to and running parallel with the bridge road." While new roads emerged, other older historic ones like the Great Wagon Road disappeared, having served their purpose.

During the 1850s and 1860s, petitions were regularly filed and granted for what were called cartways; as the name indicates, it was designed as a way for a farmer to get a wagon of produce to market. Furthermore, the law stated that when a cartway was used to go to and from church, it could never be blocked or discontinued.

This period saw rapid changes in human traffic as well, primarily as the children and grandchildren of the early pioneer families fled for new lands. It was in their blood to keep moving on. This outmigration had the effect of continuously making land available in the Yadkin Valley to another wave of settlers, gladly willing to settle for land already cleared and plowed.

For half a century, immigrants from north to south had ridden or walked along the Appalachian Mountain Range and wondered what was on the other side. Dr. Thomas Walker of Virginia was among the first to get there in 1750, going through the southwesternmost settlement in Virginia. He and a few companions followed the most trampled paths they could find, where Indians and animals had met with the least resistance. They discovered a narrow, rocky pass in the mountains that rewarded them with a view of the other side. This defile (the odd name for a narrow geographic opening) was immediately recognized for what it was—the gateway to the other side—and the Cumberland Gap entered history. It was, like the Shallow Ford in the mountains, the way to get across.

Today, one can make his way through the Cumberland National Park and discover what the pioneers did and see why it was so critical. A small narrow path still exists with the gap at a peak. Descending either side away from it, it is obvious one is on the other side of a great divide.

Many people mistakenly believe that Daniel Boone discovered the Cumberland Gap, but he merely created a good use for it. He first heard of it from John Findlay when the two served together in the French and Indian War. Salisbury lawyer Richard Henderson, who had shrewdly bought up tracts of yet-unseen land given as payment to soldiers for their service in the war, offered two thousand acres to Boone to cut a trail settlers could

Cumberland Gap.
Courtesy of author.

use to traverse and then buy land from him there. In 1769, a mere twenty years since Morgan Bryan had first led his extended family across Shallow Ford into the Forks of the Yadkin, his grandson-in-law led the first group of settlers into Kentucky.

This was colossal. The Great Wagon Road continued to carry people south but now a branch of it took a hard turn to the west, opening up a new western frontier in an ongoing process in American history. The West provided a release valve of sorts even as the War for Independence was beginning. Those with politically incorrect loyalties or just wanting to avoid the fight had a place to flee and the American West became the place of second chances.

This new branch of the Great Wagon Road became known as Boone's Road or the Kentucky Road or the Wilderness Road, but regardless, it was the Way West. A new generation of Americans was about to be shaped by yet another place to tame and claim. James Knox Polk, bearing in his name his Scottish heritage, and Abraham Lincoln and his son Thomas were among the first followers of Boone, becoming part of the story of another future president bearing his grandfather's name. One church family moved together as a group, with their minister leading them in song as well as in prayer along the way. It might have seemed that all of central North Carolina was emptying out were it not for the masses still coming south. Pioneers in Kentucky had some of the same challenges their parents had—the threat of the Indians, starting over in an unestablished area and clearing land—but many of them had done it before as children. The frontier in the forks of the Yadkin River had prepared the next generation to do it in the West. The old soil of the Yadkin Valley became the seedbed for a new land.

In the first U.S. Census taken in 1790, it was counted that 70,000 people had made that leap of faith over the mountains in the mere twenty-one years since Daniel Boone looked back over his shoulder and said, "C'mon." By the 1800 census, those living west of the mountains had tripled, doubled again by the one in 1810 and topped 500,000 by 1820 (when the total population of the nation was less than 10 million), the last census in Daniel Boone's lifetime. Not all but many of those peopling the trans-Appalachian West had crossed Shallow Ford one last time to head toward the Cumberland Gap.

Daniel stayed long enough to ask the Kentucky Assembly to be given the job of widening the road to thirty feet with this appeal: "I am No Statesman, I am a Woodsman and think My Self as Capable of Marking and Cutting the Rode as any other man." He got no argument. Daniel eventually could see the smoke from other cabins in Boonesborough, though, and continued to move west until his death at age eighty-five in Missouri, where he finally stopped moving after burying Rebecca there. He ran out of time but never new land to explore.

There was a lot of news to be read, and more and more, people could. The citizens of the United States were becoming dramatically more literate. The first newspaper west of the Yadkin River was the *North Carolina Mercury and Salisbury Advertiser*, which began printing in 1799 in the county seat of Rowan. The newspaper business boomed in the next century as it became the literary educator of the new nation. The 1840s U.S. Census was the first to ask if a person could read and write. (It was not until the 1870 census that the questions differentiated between reading and writing, which are different skills.) This reflected a boom in reading and book production, the impetus for a cultural revolution.

Previously, the ability to read and access to the printed word were privileges that belonged exclusively to the rich, but this changed with the increase of mass printing in the 1840s. Burgeoning schools, spelling books and the necessity to conduct business in life on paper reaped a huge shift in literacy.

Reading before the printing revolution was primarily a communal activity, where one reads aloud to others. From the Old Testament scriptures being read aloud in Jewish synagogues to Daniel Boone reading *Gulliver's Travels* to his companions around a campfire, it was a skill to be shared. With the exploding increase of printed materials that included magazines and newsletters, people started reading alone, to themselves. It was a very self-contained pleasure that allowed them to be the arbitrators of information that they then shared in letters and conversation. As Beth Barton Schweiger wrote in her fascinating book *A Literate South*, "Print carried an authority that outweighed its fragile form. Even in its brief life it offered notions that lodged in people's heads and were intriguing enough to repeat in the churchyard or report in a letter or journal." Hence a person would become known as a reader, such as Armstrong "Strong" Thomasson, who lived in northern Iredell County his entire life and was known to be a voracious reader; he could be seen reading while driving his farm wagon. Communities of readers were emerging all over the region and newspapers were begun and later libraries to share books. Libraries are a hallmark of an American society that believes that knowledge should be made available to all citizens, regardless of ability to pay.

Schools began to spring up often in proximity to rivers. On the western side of the Yadkin River, just south of Shallow Ford, the Methodists took up offerings to finance a Cokesbury School (named after Bishops Coke and Asbury) in an impressive large log structure built overlooking the river by Francis Asbury's visit in 1795. Asbury described the building in his journal as "twenty feet square, two stories high, well set out with doors and windows…stands on a beautiful eminence and overlooks the Lowlands and the river Yadkin." The school was short-lived but the building served as a Methodist meeting house for a while, proving that a river location alone was no longer a guarantee of success. Hardy Jones, on whose land it had been built, soon moved to a more populous place farther north known as Martinsborough. The school thrived, as did the town of Jonesville, renamed for the teacher.

In 1857, the Yadkin College, named for the river it sat astride, was begun in Davidson County, founded by the Methodist Protestant Church. The

Davie County Library bookmobile. *Digital Davie.*

college's rural isolation and the events of the Civil War meant it always struggled, and it eventually became a college preparatory high school before closing early in the twentieth century. High Point University is considered to be the successor of that academic endeavor.

To the west, on the outskirts of Statesville, the Bethany Presbyterian Church opened Ebenezer Academy in a log cabin in 1822, and it would continue for the better part of the next eighty years. With a curriculum that focused on English, grammar and geography, it was intentionally college preparatory—pretty radical on what had been frontier not much earlier. Young Thomas Clingman of later fame would be educated there.

A Presbyterian minister made his own contribution. Born in Guilford County, Salem resident Calvin Henderson Wiley was the state's first superintendent of schools and wrote a unique textbook called the *North Carolina Reader*. While most textbooks originated in New York City, this one taught children about their own Old North State beginning in 1851; it was reprinted for many years. It taught pronunciation of North Carolina towns, rivers and native tribes and the state's rich history. Describing the Upland regions of North Carolina, Wiley wrote in 1855, "In very humble log-cabins by the wayside, you will find the walls garnished with files of newspapers; and you will find every member of the family well versed in the news and politics of the day." The log cabins of the century before were still there, filling up with print.

While many churches started their own colleges, Revolutionary War hero William R. Davie not only wrote the legislative bill but also outlined the classical curriculum for the first public university in the nation, the University of North Carolina. In the 1790s, UNC became the only American public university to grant degrees in the same century that the nation was born. Education was very important in the Old North State and it led the United States in making education available to all its citizens.

Educational opportunities for Black residents, sadly, lagged far behind. In 1918, a two-classroom Rosenwald School House was built in Yadkinville and then a second one in the Courtney community as part of a program by Booker T. Washington and Julius Rosenwald (of Sears, Roebuck), enabling the deeply valued tradition of education. North Carolina would have more Rosenwald schools—787 of them with 10 of them in Iredell County—than any other state, built in the fifteen years before the Great Depression in many small towns like Mocksville and Cooleemee.

The Old South was taking shape, but there was another revolution, a spiritual one, redefining its culture. On an autumn day in 1784, a handful of in present Davidson County. They were the remnants of a church that had been deeply disturbed by the Regulators War and the brutal execution of one

Cooleemee Rosenwald School. *Digital Davie.*

of their own, Benjamin Merrill. Their first pastor, John Gano, had taken his family back to New Jersey for safety. The stress on the church was too much, and having begun in 1758, it ceased to meet during the revolution. Thirteen Brothers and two Sisters gathered for the express purpose of reconstituting the Jersey Baptist Church. They wrote down their proceedings in a small leather journal, listing their names as an act of commitment. They also agreed on three "necesetys purchased for the church," which included one blank book, no doubt the journal in which these proceedings were recorded, as well as a gallon of wine and, yes indeed, a second gallon of wine. This was no half-hearted revival of their beloved congregation—they were prepared for a robust communion. That little gem of a journal survives in the holdings of the Special Collections at Wake Forest University library, and the church continues today. Fifteen survivors invested in history and spiritual revival. They were not alone.

The hallmark of the churches in the South in this new nation was the wide variety among them and congregational autonomy. This freedom of spirit was captured in the first sentence of the 1790 church covenant of Eatons Baptist Church in Davie County, which states, "We desire to walk together in the fear of God, through the assistance of his holy spirit."

From the earliest days of settlement, the Piedmont region of North Carolina had been a diverse landscape of church activity. The initial settlers were running away from a lot, but not church bonds. Several notable groups came here not just with their church intact but because of it, escaping the Old World's formal church pressure to conform.

Quakers had substantial membership early in the colony. Their founder, George Fox, preached in the Albemarle area in 1672. However, many others had left that church after being ostracized by the Quakers' rigid membership rules; the result was that no evidence exists that a Quaker meeting house was ever organized in the vicinity of Shallow Ford. Instead, the Quakers seem to have found and even founded other churches, most often Baptist. Records of the Bryans supporting the Separatist Baptist church plant Timber Ridge Baptist Church are multiple. Even when former Quakers did not join another church, they often had their children baptized in other churches.

The Quaker settlers were welcomed as peace-loving, hardworking neighbors, but their strict laws regarding dress, marriage and taking up arms in time of war did not result in many converts. As a new century emerged in 1800, they seemed stuck in the previous one. Their hard line on "marrying out" of their church in the long run resulted in their youth departing and their membership decreasing. They were exclusive in an evangelistic era.

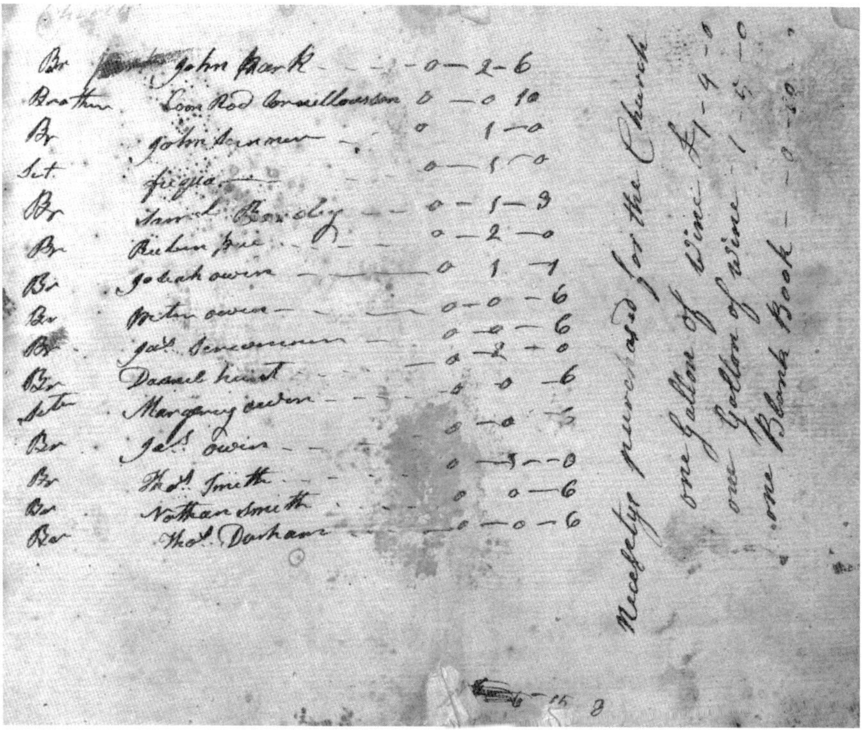

Jersey Baptist Church minutes of 1784. *Special Collections & Archives, Wake Forest University.*

Deep Creek Friends Meeting House in Yadkin County is an extant example of a Quaker community that has worshiped and survived as a congregation, albeit a dwindling one, since it first met in 1789. As time wore on, the Quakers became a puzzlement to their neighbors and were considered a peculiar people.

Presbyterianism, the church of the Scot Highlanders and Scots-Irish, most maintained its Old World rituals. Doctrinally, the Presbyterians, Baptists, Methodists and even Moravians did not dramatically differ. Uniqueness developed out of their own Reformation stories and their differences on church polity, a byproduct of their newfound freedom. However, formality began to appear cold in comparison with the Methodist zeal.

The Moravians of Wachovia are the best example of a church escaping European conformity. The Unitas Fratum (Latin for United Brethren), as they called themselves, believed that they were on a divine mission to this part of the world. They ultimately built six towns, but Salem was always the centerpiece. Bethabara was meant to be a temporary settlement, and

Bethania was a compromise as a mixed community. Friedland and Freidburg were farming communities.

The Hope community stands out because instead of a German or biblical name, it used a simple four-letter English word, and for good reason. A Maryland group asked to relocate to Wachovia following conversion when a Moravian preacher ministered the Word to them. They embodied the goal of the Moravians to infiltrate the existing community, the opposite of a cult that demands complete capitulation. A member did not have to be German or even speak the language to be a Moravian. So, Hope was an English-speaking church community within a German cultural community that was itself surrounded by a larger English colony. What Hope had in common with the other Moravian towns was not heritage or language but rather a shared belief in obedience to scriptural truth in doctrine and practice. Scott Rohrer's book *Hope's Promise* tells the fascinating story of this unique congregation of English Moravians.

The Moravians were unique among Reformation churches with their strong mission compunction. They undertook a mission to the Cherokee Indians and became the first to teach the tribe the English language in a school in Spring Place, Georgia. They also moved with the tribe when forced to relocate on the famous Trail of Tears; to this day, they are greatly honored by the Cherokee people. Surprisingly, they did not have much impact outside the immediate area around Wachovia. Ultimately, the Moravians were most successful in their missions outreach in Africa, and today four out of five Moravians are African.

Following the Revolution, Methodists began to make serious inroads into the communities along the Yadkin River. Methodists were a small fringe group until the Wesley brothers, John the preacher and Charles the hymn writer, and George Whitefield traveled around the colonies preaching. The colonial Methodists were issued their own independent charter in 1784, a fitting act for a new church in a new nation. Not just another transplant, it became an organic American church. In half a century, the Methodist church had become the largest religious group in the country.

British Methodist Francis Asbury came to America from England in 1771 at age twenty-six, never had a wife and family or even his own home and traveled on horseback or foot around the American frontier over the next forty-five years, holding meetings wherever allowed. Having planned to stay a decade, the War for Independence made it difficult to return, and he remained here the rest of his life and became an American citizen.

Asbury averaged about five thousand miles per year traveling around the South and West, literally living out of his saddlebags. Uneducated for the ministry (he studied Greek and Hebrew on horseback as he traveled), he spoke as the common man to common men. He was perfect for the small communities of central North Carolina and the frontier settlements of Kentucky. Years after he died, a statue of him on horseback was erected in Washington, D.C., the capital of an adopted country that practiced separation of church and state; it is, according to the D.C. Historic Sites website, a "rare example of a commemoration of a religious leader in DC."

A vast amount is known about the travels and travails of Asbury because he kept a journal. His vivid descriptions of treacherous river crossings and ferries ("Ah! The ferries! We shall have them, sink or swim") and particularly fords give insight. He remembered harrowing times when he believed that he would be killed or lose valuable books to the water; he dreaded these encounters so much that he wrote of going miles out of the way to avoid them. Given the routes he described, Francis Asbury must have crossed the Shallow Ford multiple times, but it did not get mentioned because it always provided a safe crossing. Boring is good with river crossings.

Among the places Asbury preached at in his large circuit, many were local to the Shallow Ford area. McKnight's Meeting House on current Highway 158 in Clemmons was a favorite layover with landowner George McKnight. McKnight lived to be eighty-one, and at his death, it was noted that he loved to have preaching in his home. Asbury wrote in his journal on Monday, May 19, 1788, "After riding nearly thirty miles we came to M'Knight's chapel in North Carolina. Here I preached on Peter's denial of Christ." He spoke there often and eventually held annual conferences at McKnight's Meeting House. At one such gathering of Methodist pastors in 1789, Asbury launched the first Methodist periodical printed in America, *The Arminian*. Most attendees coming from the north and west would have crossed the river at Shallow Ford.

Asbury also mentioned preaching at Morgan Bryan's (meaning in his home, as Bryan was not a pastor) on February 19, 1786, having crossed the Shallow Ford. The year 1799 saw him at Beal's Chapel. Shortly afterward, he stayed at the "widow Featherston's on Dutchman's Creek…we soon called a meeting after our arrival."

Whitaker Meeting House is a compelling example of how a community church where Asbury preached was formed that is still impactful today. Located at the fork in the road where old Farmington Road turned off the main road to Salem (now US Highway 158), its cemetery behind a diner is its last marker. Deed records reported, "On the 29th day of March, 1794 William Whitaker Jr. sold to the Whitaker Methodist Episcopal Church and Trustees

Francis Asbury statue. *Courtesy of author.*

1 acre of land including grave yard, meeting house, all out buildings, and church yard. For the sum of 20 shillings." This deed indicates the following: it was no doubt called Whitaker Meeting House after a landowner people would recognize; there was an organized church in place given an official name, with trustees who could sign legal documents; and they already had built and had been using a meeting house and had cleared a cemetery.

The trustees mentioned on the deed for Whitaker Meeting House included William Whitaker Jr. (other records indicate that his family arrived in Davie County forty years earlier as Quakers), Shadrick Dial (mentioned in Asbury's journals), Israel Whitaker, Nicholas Keen, William McMahan, James

Oak Grove Methodist Church. *Digital Davie.*

Noland and George Gentle. The number of deacons or trustees a church had does not always indicate its size, but it is a measuring stick, as a very small gathering might have trouble qualifying seven men. It was recorded in the Salisbury Circuit church records that the successors of the trustees must "permit those preachers known by the name of METHODIST, and no other persons to have and enjoy the free use and benefits of the Premises" and that said preacher to "preach no other doctrine that that contained in MR. JOHN WESLEY's notes upon the new TESTAMENTS and four VOLUMES OF SERMONS" (upper case emphasis from original). Whitaker Meeting House was not a general hall for any meetings but rather solely a Methodist church building. Self-determination was not just political.

Many a service was held there before it ceased to function at that spot in the mid-1830s. The descendants of Whitaker Meeting House organized two churches, each serving a concentrated community. Smith Grove Methodist Church still claims a camp meeting site. Oak Grove Methodist Church has served its immediate community since it chose its permanent name and location around 1875.

In 1787, Francis Asbury ordained Richard Allen, an ex-slave from Virginia, to become the first bishop of the African Methodist Episcopal Church. At about the same time, another group of Black Christians created the African Methodist Episcopal Zion Church, adding the biblical term

"Zion," which emphasized God's realm. The simplest distinction between them is found in origins and styles, as the first was more Eurocentric and the latter more Afrocentric.

The Baptists would make history in the Shallow Ford area. The first Baptist church west of the Yadkin River (according to church historian George Paschal), a line in the sand of sorts that separated the settled East from the frontier West, sprang up near and was sometimes referred to as Shallow Ford. The Baptist church had jumped the divide, and all Baptists west of that mark would be the spiritual descendants of that first church they called Timber Ridge Baptist Church. None of its original records are known to exist, but multiple mentions from varying sources, as well as oral histories that have survived and the remains of a small fenced cemetery on its old grounds, bear witness to its story. The first footprint of the Baptists west of the Yadkin River in the new frontier was near the Shallow Ford, where they stirred the water when they held their baptisms there.

Early missionary Shubal Stearns not only founded the Sandy Creek Baptist Church but also trained others to start mission churches, among them two brothers, William and Joseph Murphy. William Murphy preached mostly across Virginia, where the brothers began their ministry, known as "the Murphy boys." Joseph Murphy would later become the first pastor of the first Baptist church west of the Yadkin River in North Carolina, linking local Baptist heritage to the fruit of Whitefield and the Great Awakening through the person of Shubal Stearns.

Hundreds of churches were started out of Sandy Creek, with sweeping results across the Carolinas. One convert of a missionary pastor sent out by Stearns, Richard Furman, for whom the university was named, became such an outspoken leader that Cornwallis put a bounty on his head, forcing him to flee his native Charleston for a while. But he persisted in his beliefs and emphasis on education and even named two of his sons (the first one died in infancy) John Gano after the Jersey Baptist pastor he greatly admired.

Baptist pastor John Gano was closest to the Yadkin River, just east of it outside present Lexington. Gano was born in New Jersey of Huguenot descent and came south in 1755 to minister to a group of Christians in the Jersey Settlement. Jersey Baptist Church early had a substantial group of baptized members. One deacon, Benjamin Merrill, was both farmer and blacksmith; he creatively used a creek on his farm to power simple machinery that would bore out the barrel of a gun. He was known for the clever practice of starting the machine in the evening and then leaving it to work all night, to find the gun ready for the next step the following morning, before he became known for being executed by Governor Tryon in the Regulators War.

John Gano—famously credited by some church historians as the army chaplain who baptized General George Washington—went on to pastor First Baptist Church of New York City. He returned to North Carolina in 1794 after his wife died to marry Sarah Bryan, the widow of Captain Thomas Bryan, a Shallow Ford local woman he had known before and could not forget.

Moravian records revealed that Baptist ministers were traveling through and preaching at any opportunity granted as early as 1760. The Moravians wrote that "at this time the Baptists are the only ones in the country who go far and wide preaching and caring for souls." A minister of Wachovia, Richard Utley, was invited to preach on November 30, 1768, at a Baptist meeting house built on the other side of the Yadkin by Mr. Murphy, the Baptist minister. He and others frequently recorded preaching to crowds of more than two hundred. Timber Ridge Baptist Church constructed a building perhaps as early as 1768 but certainly by 1773, earlier than any other Baptist church west of the Yadkin River was known to have a regular meeting place.

Church historian Edward Morgan visited Timber Ridge Baptist Church and described a meeting house near Shallow Ford measuring thirty feet by twenty-six feet, writing that there were thirty-two members at the time it was organized. It was often referred to as Shallow Ford since that was a well-known location and because baptisms of new converts often took place at the convenient ford; sure footing in water is important in this activity, as many a baptizer has had to learn the hard way that you never immerse the candidate facing downstream lest the current carry him away. Many years later, S. Oscar Rich told of being baptized in the "baptizing hole" at Shallow Ford when he joined Farmington Baptist Church as a youth.

The Timber Ridge Baptist Church enjoyed the support of the local landowners, especially Morgan Bryan of Bryan's Settlement. Murphy once preached in a series of meetings that lasted for days and baptized Bryan's wife, Martha, at Shallow Ford (according to the Timber Ridge Diary).

The Boone family who remained in the Yadkin Valley may well have worshiped at Timber Ridge. "Old Mother Boone" (Sarah, Daniel's mother) was known throughout the area as a devout woman. While family lore says that she wore Quaker garb her entire life, even in her old age when she lived with her daughter Mary and husband, William Bryan, with no Quaker meeting house to attend she may well have been a congregant, if not actual member, of Timber Ridge Baptist Church, organized well before her death in 1777. Many of her children and grandchildren became members of Baptist churches, and a few of her grandsons were known on the Kentucky frontier as Baptist preachers. Daniel Boone never joined a formal church after his Quaker experiences, but mostly the Boones became Baptists and his wife, Rebecca, raised in the Bryan family attending Timber Ridge, was no doubt affected by this early assembly of Baptists called Timber Ridge.

A document, titled the Timber Ridge Diary, of which transcribed copies from several sources exist, identified seven Bryan couples and also mentioned three baptisms of children of the Bryans. While this level of detail mostly interests descendants or church historians, it does give credibility as well as rich details of a church family full of children becoming believers (as Baptists never practiced infant baptism).

By 1790, in the minutes of the newly organized Yadkin Baptist Association, the congregation was listed as Timber Ridge with Pastor Peter Eaton, Murphy having moved on to Deep Creek Church in Surry County. Timber Ridge reported a membership of thirty-five. Membership numbers tended to be lower than attendance as requirements to join were more demanding than today, and members were often removed for good reason. Genealogical researchers using Baptist church minutes are most likely to find their ancestors' names if they misbehaved and were good repenters, as churches took discipline very seriously. Another local Baptist church minutes told of a young man being disciplined for falling away in attendance but it was decided to be merciful and wait to hear from him after he returned from serving in the Continental army.

Pastor Peter Eaton is the only other pastor connected to the Timber Ridge Church and records of other churches tell of some trouble between him and the membership that was eventually reconciled; nonetheless, the church did not seem to survive it. Peter Eaton remained in the area, showing up in multiple legal land transactions.

Timber Ridge Baptist Church may have been located near Murphy's home or centrally located between clumps of settlers, but it seems to have stayed in the same location or proximity for its near half century of existence. Miss Flossie Martin, early collector of history for Davie County, wrote in 1955 after some research, "The property of the former Timber Ridge Baptist Church is nine miles from Mocksville, about a quarter of a mile to the left of the Winston-Salem-Mocksville highway…near the present old part of the graveyard." Miss Martin had special insight, as her great-great-grandparents were charter members of Timber Ridge Baptist Church.

Even more convincing proof of exact location comes when the church closed in 1814 and the property was sold to the Methodists, who erected a new church with the name Bethlehem. In the cemetery of Bethlehem Methodist Church on Redland Road today, in the far corner, is a monument of stones where the first preaching service of their new church was held, perhaps in the pulpit of the former Baptist meeting house that they probably would have used until building their own sanctuary. The small, old cemetery behind it has the last remains of members of Timber Ridge with the surnames of Black, James, Gordon, Smith, Lee, Call, Thomas and Cornell—makers of history simply because they wanted to have a place to hear the Bible preached. One local legend says that the logs that were dismantled from the Timber Ridge Meeting House were sold to John Bailey, who used them to construct a still. Timber Ridge Baptist Church ceased to exist after less than fifty years, but its fruit remained in other congregations. Churches, like their members, have life spans.

Timber Ridge lived on after it birthed two church plants, often the practice to reduce distance and travel time for those attending. One church plant was at Mulberry Fields in then Surry County, now Yadkin, and first called Murphy's Meeting House, as he held meetings before moving to become its pastor for the rest of his life; it would later be called Deep Creek Baptist Church by its location. The other church begun by Timber Ridge was called Forks of the Yadkin Baptist Church; it outlived its parent and is believed to have become Fork Baptist Church, organized as its own assembly of believers in 1793 and still crowning the hilltop alongside Highway 64. It is the lasting legacy of the first Baptist church west of the Yadkin.

Black Protestant churches also came into existence, as noted by Juan Williams and Quinton Dixie in their work *This Far by Faith*: "The emergence of independent black Baptist churches in the United States in the eighteenth century occurred during the effort by American colonists to eradicate British rule in the colony. On the periphery sat two critical cultural phenomena: the rise of 'revivalistic' congregational churches and the ongoing efforts to eliminate slavery. Indeed, the War for American Independence created the philosophical framework from which blacks argued that liberation was intended for *all* people."

The growing African enslaved population in the new states was also affected by Protestant churches. The Baptists even recognized the legitimacy of slave marriages. Literacy was an obstacle, especially in denominations where group readings were common practice. The Methodists in South

Fork Baptist Church. *Digital Davie.*

Carolina were the first to advocate for religious instruction for the slaves, which of necessity included teaching them how to read.

The first wave of revivals among enslaved people took place in the 1750s. Soon Black preachers came forward. Black historian John Hope Franklin wrote that this allowed Black leaders to take initiative and create churches that fit their culture. Black preachers developed their own sermon styles of rhythm and repetition to help illiterate slaves remember key points. Having been relocated by force themselves, the story of Exodus resonated with them. The old spiritual "Let My People Go" echoed through slave cabins. If ever a group needed to cling to hope, it was this one.

Indeed, by the time of the Civil War, many enslaved people lived on the hope of divine intervention, that God would deliver them. Meanwhile, the Bible gave them strength. To this day, musical spirituals, preaching style and even dress reflect their interpretation of what Christianity meant to them.

Sunday schools arose as the answer to educating converts in the Bible. They began in England, and then Sabbath Schools appeared in the 1790s in Rhode Island on this continent. By 1825, Farmington's Olive

Branch Methodist Church had begun this program to educate children and communicated in a letter to Eatons Meeting House the successes and disappointments as they considered it also.

Imprints show up in names. Churches were organized where there were communities forming and often shared the same geographic name such as Bear Creek in Davie. But the hen did not always precede the egg. Many communities in the area have a biblical name from the church at its community's core; an article in the *Raleigh News* in February 10, 1932, noted that seven of the nineteen towns in Davie County had biblical names, including Ephesus, Joppa, Jericho, Jerusalem, Macedonia, Cana and Bethlehem. One northwest corner of Davie County was called "Egypt" for a short while in 1881 when it alone had grain after a severe drought. Interestingly, the Moravian settlement's name of Bethabara in the Hebrew language meant "House of the Ford" and indicated a resting place on the east side of the River Jordan where John the Baptist was known to preach to the passersby and baptize in the conveniently located river. Mostly biblically derived church names came from the Old Testament (whose stories were exceedingly more popular and well known the nineteenth century), but there are churches with names derived from the New Testament as well, like the Gospel Way Baptist Church in Yadkin County or another—a perfectly named church for a community and the gospel that grabbed Saul's heart and made him the Apostle Paul that sits on the road to Damascus, Virginia, from Abingdon—simply called Damascus Road Baptist Church.

The culture of the old South was deeply affected by this spiritual revolution. Historian Perry Miller concluded that "the dominant theme in America from 1800 to 1865 is the invisible persistence of the revival" and that it was the "central mode of this culture's search for cultural identity." In modern times, it is uncommon to think the hand shaping American culture was extended from churches, but it could not have been in better hands.

Protestant churches popularized revivalism, which not only helped Baptists and Methodism spread but also shaped American religious life. The individualistic, democratic and fervent spirit of these revivals produced many offspring, including North Carolina native son Billy Graham, himself a convert of evangelist Mordecai Ham in a camp meeting.

In 1800, the South was about to be penetrated by the camp meetings. This grass-roots movement was an uprising within Christian culture. The preaching was hot, the response intense and the congregation supportive in the camp meetings, where hundreds gathered and camped out in lengthy revival services. They also served as reunions, great potlucks and social events, exposing young men and women to those from other neighborhoods, but all that was gravy. The meat of the movement was the evangelistic spread of the gospel.

There is an important distinction between churches and camp meetings. The early meeting houses in this area were linked to distinctive church bodies with a regular meeting in one location, primarily tied to a Protestant denomination. Camp meetings, however, were occasional, sometimes annual, mass gatherings for revival services that often featured preachers and attendees from multiple churches. They were a unique, revival-driven event, not an enduring church body.

Church history tells that the camp meeting movement began in Kentucky in June 1799, when the McGhee brothers were preaching in a meeting house at Gaspar River. When it became so crowded that listeners spilled outside, so did the service. This might have been something beginning in the West and then spreading back to the East except that the preachers, John and William McGhee, had grown up along the Yadkin River near Salisbury, so the story really began by the banks of the Yadkin. One was a Methodist and one was a Presbyterian but they agreed on the need for revival.

No fewer than a dozen camp meetings have been identified in the Shallow Ford area, and a multitude of local churches have their origins in brush arbor camp meetings. Olive Branch Methodist Church moved from a camp meeting to become a church in 1806 when it purchased land from Robert and Nancy Fields. Among its early pastors were two named Quakin Love and Lemon Shell (impossible to make this stuff up). Olive Branch Methodist Church moved up the road and became Farmington Methodist in 1882 but left a legacy in its cemetery on Farmington Road and its storied contribution to the Farmington community. Farmington gave the church a young man named Moses Brock, who preached his first sermon in a neighbor's house. In 1820, he joined the Methodist Conference and for the next forty years was instrumental in establishing churches across the South.

Ward's Campground was almost within sight of the Shallow Ford on the river. This no doubt made traveling from the eastern side of the river convenient for attendees, as well as the proximity to baptize. Few camp meeting structures survive because they were not built to be permanent. An exception is Center Methodist Church Arbor in Davie County, which still hosts events in its historic timber frame arbor built in 1876, the last physical testament to a long history of camp meetings where sounds of music and shouts of "Amen" filled the air.

Arbor Camp Meeting. *Digital Davie.*

Traveling evangelists joined local pastors in preaching. Stories of challenging crossings at Shallow Ford were common by these traveling itinerant preachers on their way to and from camp meetings. One was written by Robert Paine in an old, rare book, *Life and Times of William McKendree*, when he was traveling with the Methodist bishop in 1824. After waiting two days for the flooded Yadkin River to subside, they decided that they had to find a way across. His account reads, "Ascertaining that there was a large canoe dug out of the body of a large tree lying a mile or two above, we presently got it floated down and quickly carried all of the baggage and equipment across…then the horses swam over by the side of our craft, and finally the carriage was placed astride it and carried over." Half a century later, in 1874, a Methodist Circuit Riding preacher named Jesse Lee almost drowned when he tried to cross Shallow Ford in rushing water. He and his horse were trapped in cragged rocks, encumbered by a heavy coat and saddlebag. He was delivered but the Methodists were not faint of heart when on a mission.

Camp meetings were first and foremost a religious activity for the masses of common farmers and workers. This was the church adjusting to the frontier population with the straight-forward speaking and lyrical singing the average person could understand. Life was hard and filled with tedium, but who better to offer a respite than the church that offered salvation and redemption? It was a marriage made in heaven, which was also on offer.

Offering heaven was at the core of the camp meetings. Where else might the converted bring their neighbors to hear the gospel to obtain forgiveness and eternal hope? Camp meetings brought the truth to the seekers, who feared no repercussions for repentance among fellow repenters. Conversions were encouraged at altar calls. One only needed to walk the sawdust trail and be enthusiastically greeted at the other end. Evangelism was the responsibility of Christianity in this new free church society, where no one was required to join or attend a church; the church must reach out and find the seeker.

The camp meetings also reaped unity of thought and spirit in a community—never completely, of course, but imagine a town where everyone heard the same sermons together. Frenchman Alexis de Tocqueville traveled around the new nation in the 1830s and investigated what made it great. His conclusion, printed in *Democracy in America*, was that America would be great as long as its churches were strong: "I do not know whether all American[s] have a sincere faith in their religion—for who can search the human heart—but I am certain that they hold it to be indispensable to the maintenance of republican institutions." The new Americans were learning their role of becoming self-governing citizens and were being schooled by preachers.

Even the music changed. Lyrics like "On Jordan's stormy banks I stand and cast a wistful eye to Canaan's fair and happy land" used common imagery to represent spiritual experiences. Who among them could not remember standing on the banks of a stormy Yadkin River and casting a wistful eye across the Shallow Ford? This particular song, one of the most popular of the era, was written in 1787 by English Baptist pastor Stephen Stennett but found its footing in American camp meetings, where the refrain "I am bound for the Promised Land" was added by pioneers.

Music was a key element in camp meetings. Those blessed with an organ in their homes would often transport it on a wagon to provide support. The ability to read music was not a requirement, however, as simple choruses could be learned in group singing. Often new words were put to a familiar secular tune already well known. The result was that people began to sing on their way to meetings, sang more during the services and sang again on their way back home. Theology had staying power in a tune they could not get out of their heads.

A tune book, *The Southern Harmony*, written by "Singin' Billy" Walker from Spartanburg, South Carolina, and printed in 1835, was sold in general stores ("On Jordan's Stormy Banks" was in it). A school of music developed in the Appalachian Mountains that taught an alternative to those who could not read music: shape-note reading, where the note did not represent one note but rather the relationship to the prior note and the steps between. What better tool for understanding music than making it about relationships? This lasted well into the twentieth century, when local Methodist church youth groups would travel to learn shape-note singing from Brother Leslie in the mountains. Familiar hymns were printed in hymnbooks for the Baptists by Andrew Broaddus, himself a convert during the revivals of the 1780s after overhearing the compelling singing of a Baptist meeting. Cambridge University Press recently wrote in the online article "Hymnody as History," "The hymns of evangelical Protestantism are the most widely used spiritual texts in American history."

Camp meeting was not a spectator sport. It provided communal singing, praying together and fellowship. It accommodated frontier life, where neighbors often lived miles away and rarely interacted with one another. Seasonal camp meetings became the Christian community gathering together. News was exchanged, new babies were drooled over and kisses were stolen.

Places that were suitable for hosting camp meetings—a large enough clearing and a good source of water like a river or creek—were returned to time and time again. Still today, on a warm country evening, camp meetings can be heard on the back roads in the South. A local couple recently rode up into the mountains to a small town that hosted a camp meeting years before. When they stopped at the only gas station to ask for directions to the camp meeting in town, the response was, "Which one?"

The South runs on guilt for good reason. Sin was condemned, the devil and his works were rebuked and all praise turned toward a sovereign God. Hope was held out in conversion on an individual basis. Redemption did not depend on family connections or church membership—perfect for people who had often left both behind. Life might be hard but it was brief and heaven awaited. Camp meeting was creating a culture, one redeemed sinner at a time.

Camp meetings were the breeding ground of a new culture, prompted by a spiritual revolution. They were communal and welcoming, with attendees addressing one another as "Brother" and "Sister" if of the faith (and not just because the name escaped them). All the characteristics associated with the Old South stemmed from camp meetings—warm, friendly, helpful, respectful and kind. Striking up a friendly conversation with a stranger. Expressive folk music and storytelling. Volunteering to sing in the choir or usher. Hospitality and porch sitting to connect with neighbors. Giving in the offering plate or donation box. A heartfelt "How ya doin'?" Throwing up a hand in a wave or in worship. Praying in public and mounting "In God We Trust" on the courthouse. Sharing food at a potluck. Believing that all saints and sinners walk on the same level ground like the sawdust trail in a camp meeting tent. Recognize this place?

CIVIL WAR

A teenage girl stood on the porch tying her bonnet on a warm day in the spring of 1865 in the small town of Cana, transfixed by a sequence of flashing lights. Lizzybeth asked Elminy, the enslaved kitchen worker making donuts, to walk with her to where she could see them better. What they saw was a cloud of dust, indication of a large group on horseback, and Lizzy recalled that her first thought was, "Company and the house in a mess." She had all the makings of a good guilt-ridden southern woman. Elminy answered, "Oh Good Lord Jesus, dat ain't no company...dems...dems...git in dat house!" After the riders rode in and dismounted, Lizzybeth recognized that they were part of Stoneman's troops, the enemy, but thought, "Why they look just like anyone else."

Lizzy heard a commotion down in the geese pen, where Elminy had three old settin' geese on nests. "I looked down the wall and saw a young, towheaded soldier coming toward the kitchin leadin' his horse with one arm and his hat curved in the crook of his arm. To my astonishment I realized he had it full of geese eggs." He promptly commanded Elminy to cook them up, even as she protested. While he and a few others studied a map, she boiled them and delivered them to the soldiers. The same soldier put them in his haversack, and then they left. Lizzie thought that Elminy was crying, but she was laughing so hard that tears rans down her face while she spilled out, "Dey got dem eggs from de old settin' goose, Miss Lizzie—dey is pure rotten." This story was told by Elizabeth Frost Cain firsthand and captured the rude awakenings that the Civil War had in store.

In the big picture, the Civil War was the defining event in the life of a young republic. The world was watching to see if this new form of government would work in a crisis or be torn asunder. In the smaller arena, the Shallow Ford area would be devastated before it was over.

History has the benefit of knowing the outcome of any crisis. That was not granted to the rural farmers and small towns in the newly formed counties of Yadkin, Davie and Forsyth in Piedmont North Carolina in 1860 when faced as communities and individuals with a wrenching decision. These were the children and grandchildren of veterans of the Revolutionary War, freedom fighters who had gambled everything to become Americans. Southerners had a deeply ingrained chivalry that rallied to the notion of defending one's homeland. They would summon the courage to do it again, to break free of a controlling government and start over with a new ruling force—if the right to do so was first won on the battlefield.

Trouble had already been created by Davie County native Hinton Helper's abolitionist book, *The Impending Crisis of the South*, circulated as contraband. Helper came from a slave owning family and later wrote racist books, but he claimed to speak on behalf of the poor who did not own slaves and to make the case for the economic pitfalls of slavery for farmers in the South. The book was distributed by abolitionists before Lincoln's election and heatedly debated in the U.S. Congress, as well as banned in North Carolina. Helper became a traitor in his home state.

The Civil War was accurately named, as civilians became soldiers and fellow Americans fought one another. More American casualties occurred during the Civil War than all other military conflicts in its history combined because the combatants were all Americans. The cause of the Civil War is debatable, but ultimately the question at stake was whether the Southern states would be allowed to depart.

Secession was the first step, severing political allegiance to the lawmakers of the United States who were threatening to outlaw slavery. Secession was not a novel idea. New York City threatened to secede as the war was hurting its commerce, prompting President Lincoln to quip that its departure would not be unlike the front door setting up housekeeping by itself. Secession was always a bold statement of self-determination, but in the end, both sides had to agree for it to become reality.

The Civil War that would plunder the lives of Americans around Shallow Ford was not inevitable. Having spent decades avoiding it, principals were still trying to diffuse the political tension. In the days between Lincoln's election and inauguration, President James Buchanan was diligently negotiating with southern congressmen. The final meeting was planned and then canceled at the last minute when none other than Congressman Jefferson Davis brought word to Buchanan that Anderson had occupied Fort Sumter.

Major Robert Anderson, assigned to oversee the defense of Charleston Harbor on behalf of the United States, had owned slaves, was married to a Georgian and was certain that a resolution could be found; he was doing his job of military preparedness at Fort Sumter and hoped and prayed that hostilities could be avoided. His second in command, Abner Doubleday, always had his spyglass ready and kept meticulous records of the efforts to avoid armed conflict. (Yes, *that* Abner Doubleday, who supposedly invented baseball. This detailed diarist never mentioned the game and had moved away from his hometown by 1839 but was credited with it in place of another local named Abner, who killed his wife and was committed to an insane asylum. Doubleday did enjoy the game and always made sure that soldiers were supplied with balls and bats.)

On the Confederate side of the bay in Charleston, defensive measures and cadets from The Citadel were prepared by General P.G.T. Beauregard, whose favorite teacher and mentor in military school had been Robert Anderson, out commanding Fort Sumter. Meanwhile, Beauregard's sons back in Louisiana were attending a school supervised by William Tecumseh Sherman. The Civil War divided friends.

Beauregard also exercised restraint and repeatedly sent his chief aide, Captain James Chesnut, out in a rowboat with peace treaties. Chesnut's now more well-known wife, Mary, was frantically keeping her own diary, which would give insight into the frivolity leading up to war, with such great expressions as one woman's when word arrived Lincoln had been elected: "That settles the hash!" Chesnut's last trip across the bay was at 3:30 a.m. on April 12 and firing commenced from the Charleston side an hour later.

The Civil War started off in a very civil way. It was not a fair fight with the Federals who had twenty-one cannons, only eighty soldiers and a few laborers (it is a very small island) greatly outmatched by the Confederates' forty-eight cannons and seven thousand troops. Beauregard wrote that when Anderson fired back, the Confederate gunners cheered, "Anderson for his gallantry, although themselves still firing upon him." Beauregard was quirky: he was a huge fan of Napoleon and also filed for a patent for seeds that he swore could cure bites by mad dogs, provided they were consumed with a large amount of sherry—it was not taken seriously. Beauregard, who commanded the first shots of the war to be fired, was also one of the last on the ground in Stoneman's Raid. He served for the duration of the long war.

The war that had been simmering for decades in the halls of Congress had begun between friends on a Carolina morning over water and would end in the Carolina mountains between enemies.

Not all North Carolinians were as giddy over secession as their Southern counterpart. Seen as advantageous to slaveholding plantation owners in the east, yeoman farmers in the hinterlands west of the Yadkin feared that they would suffer the effects most for slaves they did not own. They were not wrong.

On May 21, five months after South Carolina, North Carolina left the Union. No rush to judgment and certainly no consensus, but once the lot had been cast, most citizens got on board out of a sense of duty.

North Carolina's governor when the war began, John Willis Ellis, was the descendant of Rowan County settlers along the Yadkin River (one of the oldest tombstones west of the river near Shallow Ford was that of his ancestor John Ellis, buried in 1753). Governor Ellis studied law under Richmond Mumford Pearson in Mocksville, practiced law in Salisbury, married a neighbor there (who died weeks later) and was elected to the state legislature, where he championed the expansion of railroads and the rights of the insane. He served on the Superior Court of North Carolina before being elected governor in 1858. In April 1861, Governor Ellis famously refused President Lincoln's request for North Carolina troops to fight for the Union and instead sent them to confiscate Federal posts and the arsenal at Fayetteville. Three months later, he was dead at age forty, having quickly left his mark on his home state at a critical time in its history.

There was no turning back. The early conflict remained along the Carolina coast at a small, recently named village of Secessionville and then Cape Hatteras in North Carolina. During 1863, there were no major battles in North Carolina. There was resentment among some western farmers for the impressment of food and supplies for a Confederate army that they never saw.

Many boys from local counties crossed Shallow Ford to muster into the Confederacy. Without North Carolina's contribution in manpower, the Confederacy could not have fought the war as long as it did. The state contributed more in troops and resources than any other state, approximately 125,000 men engaged in the conflict—more than the number of registered voters in the state. The vast majority were volunteers, not conscripts. This number was nearly one-sixth of the Confederate army, and in the final two years, nearly 50 percent of Lee's army were North Carolinians. North Carolinians earned their nickname as Tar Heels during the Civil War—

A.A. Anderson, Davie County soldier. *Digital Davie.*

first as an insult, but they claimed they at least stuck to their places in the fight. In an 1863 Raleigh newspaper article, a Confederate soldier from North Carolina wrote, "The troops from other States call us 'Tar Heels.' I am proud of the name," as North Carolinians have been ever since.

All the tragedy of a civil war aside, it created great inconvenience. North Carolinians prior to secession received their mail delivered by the U.S. Postal Service. That abruptly stopped. Among the other duties the newly formed government of the Confederacy assumed, it had to find a way to get mail to people. Historian E. Merton Coulter observed that "no Confederate activity, outside of raising armies, touched the ordinary citizen so closely" as ensuring mail delivery. Rural post offices like the ones at Huntsville, Farmington and Clemmons were hubs of information in a community. With so many men away from home serving in the army, mail was necessary, for morale alone.

Letters home served not only as news and reassurance to relatives but also often as last words to wives and children. Sadly, many letters written from camp the night before a battle would arrive after the family received word of the death of the soldier who had penned it. Yadkin native Private Abner Stokes Haire wrote frequent letters to his wife, Ellan. He wrote of four letters from her waiting for him when he arrived at a camp in Goldsborough, of getting the garden plowed and corn planted if she could, of the awful camp food and of forgiveness for words she had spoken but mostly of love: "I don't want to see nobody Els in the world but you and my little boy. I got the print of his hand and the lock of his hair you sent me." His last letter, written on May 28, 1862, less than a month before he was wounded and died, ended with, "May the Lord be with you all I bin out of paper I close my letter Your affectionat husband til death Bless you."

No wonder many chose to avoid the war. The backwoods became hiding place for fugitives—Confederate deserters, escaped prisoners of war and unionists. Wilkes County was known as a unionist hotbed (called "Ol' U.S."), easily found by following the Yadkin River at night; many a farmer made a morning discovery that he was missing some eggs or a horse. Shallow Ford undoubtedly was a stage for the furtive glances and hurried movements of someone on the run.

Then there were the bushwhackers, named for obvious reasons. One bushwhacker was shot in the bushes beside Forbush Baptist Church in Yadkin County, where brothers Isaac and Franklin Groce went to great lengths to avoid conscription. When Isaac was captured by the Home Guard and was being transported to prison in Salisbury, he escaped and vowed never to be captured again. Ida, as he was known, became a leader of a gang that aggressively dogged the Home Guard. One story passed down through the family to writer Ernest Clarence Groce told of a summer night when Ida and his gang crept into a house where the guards were sleeping and stole their gun belts slung over the bedposts, loosened their horses and fired a parting shot through the floor before disappearing into the night. Not all battles were fought on battlefields.

Desertion was often just a time out to take care of family business or farming duty, after which the soldiers planned to return, making it hard for commanders to know their numbers but also reluctant to punish when they might come back. Wiley Gaither from Mocksville came home long enough to make a will once he recognized that he needed one for his family; he did and the photo he had made before his death showed in his eyes the awareness of what he faced. A cobbler came home to Huntsville to make his children much-needed shoes. When the Home Guard showed up, his children told them that he was in Goose Heaven. They left thinking they meant he was dead, but Goose Heaven was the name of a gulley where he was finishing the shoes. He then returned to his post. Davie County native and historian Hugh Lefler estimated the number of deserters at twenty-three thousand soldiers (20 percent, very similar to other states on both sides), but more than eight thousand returned, treating it more like unapproved leave.

Conscription, or the draft, was a hotly debated issue. The most vocal opponent was a local man and North Carolina Supreme Court chief justice. Judge Richmond Mumford Pearson was born in Davie County (son of the fist fighter in the revolution) and established a law school first in Mocksville and later on his plantation Richmond Hill in northern Yadkin County, where he taught the next generation of North Carolina leaders using the Socratic method of asking questions. He built a substantial brick home and outbuildings for students on land near the northern bend in the Yadkin River, preserved today as the Richmond Hill and Law School Nature Park—a remote, quiet place for learning and reflection then and now. Pearson alternated between his responsibilities on the state supreme

Richmond Mumford Pearson. *Digital Davie.*

court and debating issues of constitutionality with his students. He taught more than one thousand students, including three who later served on the court with him, two future chief justices, three state governors and three future U.S. congressmen. The legal and political future of the state of North Carolina was shaped on this peaceful hilltop by the Yadkin River in the midst of a war.

Pearson fought the governor over the constitutionality of forcing military service on men. He issued many a writ for men arrested in violation of the law. The Home Guard had the responsibility of finding draft dodgers and deserters and were resented for hounding and shaming men not in uniform. It strained many friendships.

Fifteen men in Yadkin County avoided conscription by hiding in Bond School House, ironically the original meeting house of the pacifist Deep Creek Friends. Four men were killed by the Home Guard, who, knowing that they were outnumbered, fired into the building without giving a chance to surrender. A gun battle ensued in a schoolhouse—it was a low point for morale. Killed were Magistrate James West and John Williams, both respected local citizens. All but three of the draft dodgers escaped, showed up at Judge Richmond Pearson's home nearby and were sent away as free men. Many complained that Pearson's position encouraged desertion. But he was the only government official to hold the same position in North Carolina state government before, during and after the Civil War. When all the state offices were vacated as part of the terms of surrender, he was reelected to the Supreme Court of North Carolina.

After Bond School, a number of boys decided to head for the mountains to enlist with the Union troops. A few froze to death. Two brothers, Bill and Lee Willard, were captured, tried and sentenced to be hanged as deserters in Winston-Salem. The day before the execution, their sister Grace brought a particularly large pound cake to them with files and hacksaws hidden inside. They sawed their way to freedom and escaped into the night. After the war, they returned home, married local girls and lived out their lives near Nebo. Other deserters were known to cut off fingers, claim to be slaves if dark skinned and dress as women (birth records in family Bibles were changed to hide males in the family).

The counties along the Yadkin River saw many of their young men off to fight in the war in places like Gettysburg and Atlanta. Most returned home and avoided telling the horrors of war to their children. There were no battlefields in this part of North Carolina until George Stoneman brought the war to the Piedmont, not to claim land or conquer an army but to destroy supplies of use to the Confederate army and to make the homefront feel the scourge of war. Stoneman's Raid, known locally as the "Yankee Invasion," brought the war to the citizens of this quiet corner of the South when it was almost over. The bullet had almost been dodged.

George Stoneman was a career military man. He first trained to be a surveyor and taught school. He then entered the military academy, and the rest is history—although it almost was not. When Stoneman emerged at the closing curtain of the Civil War in the South after a military career of two decades, he was desperately looking for a legacy and the redemption of his reputation. History would judge.

Stoneman's first military job was to escort Mormons migrating west, after which he went to fight the Mexicans. George Stoneman was not particularly outgoing or skilled and even clumsy. Early in his military career, he lost the end of this thumb in a gun accident; missing this finger on his dominant hand did not bode well for an armed soldier. Adding insult to injury, he was plagued with a most awkward medical condition of hemorrhoids, delicately called the piles. If shooting a pistol without a whole thumb was a challenge, riding a horse with the piles literally grounded him for lengthy periods of time. He actually filed for a disability discharge over it.

George Stoneman. *Library of Congress.*

Civil War historian Bruce Catton described Stoneman as "a lackluster field commander." In fact, Stoneman came to the game surrounded by bright lights and military geniuses, enough of them to split the number in half and scatter to two sides and still make his chance of the spotlight in the war iffy. He was frankly mediocre. However, he was determined to make his mark and got his chance, just as the war was almost over.

During several campaigns, Stoneman was sidelined for his embarrassing medical reason. Then General Joseph Hooker recruited him to lead a cavalry charge to cut Lee off from his supply route in Virginia. With more than ten thousand mounted soldiers, it was the largest cavalry attack that had been yet attempted. The Rappahannock River rose, and Stoneman hesitated…for two weeks. Hooker kept changing his orders to accommodate the delay. Eventually, Stoneman led his troops across the river and decided to experiment with a new tactic he had devised called "bursting shell"—the idea being that men would scatter in all directions, doing greater damage supposedly but in reality creating chaos. Hooker despaired of him.

Next, General Sherman recruited Stoneman to lead a cavalry charge as part of Sherman's plan to surround Atlanta. Stoneman had strict orders but got distracted by the possibility of freeing Andersonville Prison and fulfilled neither. Sherman would have relieved him of his command but could not as Stoneman had been taken prisoner. He held the dishonor of being the highest-ranking Union officer ever held in a Confederate prison (although quite a nice one: the racetrack clubhouse in Charleston); he returned to duty in a prisoner exchange.

Stoneman had one last chance. He proposed a raid from Tennessee to Virginia to liberate the saltworks (salt was a much-needed and fought-over commodity). As Sherman had completed his March to the Sea and was moving north through the Carolinas, he agreed that Stoneman could push in from the west, destroy supplies, perhaps distract Confederate troops and maybe make it as far as Salisbury. That last part appealed to Stoneman as it represented one last major prisoner of war camp waiting for him to liberate.

The war was nearing its conclusion in January 1965 when Stoneman was given permission to rally troops among "Home Yankees" in Tennessee and train them, taking much longer than anyone thought necessary for a plundering raid. By March, the city of Columbia was smoldering, and Sherman was heading toward Raleigh. General Grant began to wonder if Stoneman had gotten lost in the mountains; he had not yet begun his raid.

Stoneman's unorthodox ideas and hot temper combined with Southerners bent on revenge was always going to be a toxic mix. There was no battle plan, just pillaging and destroying any resource the Confederacy could use—food, fresh horses and clothing, most at that point coming from civilians. Normal warfare dictated that the military and supplies would be attacked, not homes and civilians. This new concept, total war, where the general populace felt the impact and suffered accordingly, was unexpected.

No one told the farmers that they were now fair game. There was no clear military target in this raid except for the Salisbury prison, and even that was not going to make a difference in the outcome of the war, releasing sick, weak prisoners.

By the time Stoneman organized his troops, it was the rainiest season anyone could remember. Finally, on March 21, the blue troops headed east in a fierce rainstorm, over the mountains, through narrow passes, headed for the town of Boone. There Stoneman's mounted men were met by Home Guards, who quickly did the math and fell back. A fifteen-year-old sniper named Steel Frazier started taking Stoneman's men down. At this point, the bloodthirsty cavalry was unleashed. They surprised a farmer in his field and shot him. They rode down the main street shooting at any target that presented itself. The citizens were shocked by the random pillaging and murder. The Battle of Boone was short-lived and very one-sided. As the troops left, they set fire to the jail. They took no prisoners.

Stoneman's troops moved from one community to the next, leaving destruction in their wake. The looting became so routine that residents knew what to expect. After four years, the manpower of the South had been decimated. Any armed resistance amounted to several elderly men and young boys, no match for the thousands of armed soldiers. Stoneman divided his troops, as they were not likely to encounter a fighting force but could cover more ground, destroying and foraging for food. They next headed for Wilkesboro, the first target in their raid along the Yadkin River.

Stoneman met more obstacles in the natural world than the human. Rivers especially frustrated him. He was perpetually fearful of being stranded on a riverbank. It happened to him at Rappahannock, then the Macon in Georgia and then on the Yadkin. Chris Hartley in his book *Stoneman's Raid 1865* made the observation that "George Stoneman remained stymied by the Yadkin River" and "of all the geographic obstacles, the Yadkin posed the greatest challenge." After Wilkesboro, when they sought to cross the northern portion of the Yadkin River, two regiments managed to get across before the torrential rainfall in the mountains came sweeping down. Eyewitnesses said that the river rose one foot in an hour.

Stoneman ordered the crossing to continue; a group tried and at least one died, swept downriver. Riding the horses across proved too difficult so they began to swim alongside the horses, clutching the reins. Even that failed. With Stoneman and some of his troops on one side separated from the rest on the other side, the commander lost his temper in a cussing tirade. While he was cooling his heels, some soldiers discovered a still in the woods and partook. Stoneman angrily called for a review of the troops he had with him and discovered that many of them were fall-down drunk.

The troops were forced to move for several days on parallel sides of the mighty Yadkin. So many were moving on the south side that word reached Salisbury that they were coming and General Beauregard prepared to defend the city.

While divided on opposite sides of the Yadkin, Stoneman's troops acted very differently; those on the north side in Surry County under Quaker colonel William J. Palmer foraged for what they needed but protected private property, even apologizing when forced to use fence rails for campfires. On the southern side of the river, memories spoke of them destroying the equipment at Jonesville Academy, burning factories and taking all the animals. Elkin was mostly spared and Jonesville was more devastated because they were simply on the right or wrong side of the river.

A new innovation in the Civil War was signaling with flags; being separated across a river provided the perfect chance to try it. Trained and sworn to secrecy as to their codes, the U.S. Army's Signal Corps would obtain a position on a hillside and bring out their kit's seven flags—in different sizes (determined by the distance it needed to be seen) and with different markings. Waving the correct banners sent a message that could be seen up to twenty-eight miles away to a corresponding team with field glasses. For it to work, it was necessary to know the codes. Alas, the corps were all on the same side so they signaled but the other side was clueless.

On April Fools' Day, they were still separated but were finally able to rope together some boats into a makeshift ferry. It took twelve hours to get all the troops across but Salisbury relaxed, for the time being.

Stoneman picked up new loyalists who became known as "Galvanized Yankees" (giving another meaning to a new term from 1836 where steel buckets were dipped in zinc, changing it on the outside). Stoneman's next stops were Dobson and Mount Airy, where an unusual dilemma occurred. The famous Siamese conjoined twins Eng and Chang Bunker (giving a name to the condition) had retired from the freak shows, married sisters and were farming and raising their families. Legend says that one of Stoneman's commanders drafted teamsters by having all the male residents put their names in a box, out of which he drew as many names as he needed. Supposedly, Eng was chosen, but Chang was not and would not cooperate. Both, together as always, were released from duty. There is no evidence of truth to this story but their eldest sons served as teens in the cause for the Confederacy. Chang's son Christopher Wren Bunker enlisted in the Virginia Cavalry and was later joined by Eng's son Stephen Decatur Bunker. Christopher was captured and imprisoned, where he battled

Christopher, Chang, Eng and Stephen Bunker. *National Public Radio.*

smallpox, caught rats to roast to survive and kept busy carving wooden musical instruments. Stephen was wounded but they both survived to return home. The war had devastated their fathers' previously wealthy farms, and Chang and Eng, at fifty-four years of age, returned to the shows to make money, hastening their demise together, as it could never be any other way, a few years later. So many victims of the Civil War in the South were never listed as casualties.

Telegraph messages from General Beauregard to General Robert E. Lee reported that his scouts had spotted Stoneman on March 31 passing Huntsville and going east toward Greensboro. Stoneman was introduced to Shallow Ford, which he would need later. Stoneman's Raid took an unplanned foray into Virginia, hoping that the fleeing Confederate officials could be captured. Critical railroad tracks and bridges were destroyed. News of his return to North Carolina prompted action, such as the clerk of court of Forsyth County distributing the court records among private homes in hopes that some would survive if buildings were torched.

Stoneman's troops headed for Shallow Ford as the only convenient crossing to get to Salisbury. A few local men were guarding it but quickly dispersed, as they were clearly outnumbered. The story was that they left one hundred new muskets behind, but it is questionable that a few men would have abandoned that many guns, let alone possess so many new muskets when weapons were hard to come by.

Again, Hartley put it best: "Shallow Ford was an important crossroads. From Stoneman's perspective, Shallow Ford had a strategic purpose. By crossing the river there, he gained access to the least defended route into Salisbury."

The Home Guard guarding Shallow Ford had relaxed after Stoneman headed into Virginia. General Beauregard diverted guards he had stationed at the crossing back to Salisbury. The few guardsmen left could not offer a real defense. Their resistance was intended more to delay, so items and injured soldiers could be hidden, than the hopeless goal of victory. When the troops were upon them, guards raced to defend their homes.

The local residents waited for the inevitable, knowing that their prime location by Shallow Ford meant there was no place to hide. Early on the morning of April 11, at about 2:00 a.m., a resident of Huntsville got the word that the troops were closing in. He had time to pack the family silver in the icebox under chunks of ice and spread straw over the top. General Thomas Clingman, recovering at home, and other soldiers fled rather than be taken prisoner. Then Huntsville tried to accommodate and pacify the enemy, even shoeing a horse. The Red Store and a warehouse were burned, destroying supplies for a lost cause. A widow fed officers all day long only to watch them make a campfire out of her fence rails and confiscate her last animals. They moved on to the Bitting plantation, where it was remembered the troops captured, killed or ran off all the cattle. Even the mail rider was captured, though later released.

From Huntsville, the troops headed south toward the community of Farmington. At the William Harding home, on present-day Wyo Road, two Union soldiers rode in and frightened a young girl, whose brother plowing in the field cut the horses loose and killed one of the soldiers. The home of Dr. John Clingman on Spillman Road was accosted by several Union cavalry; the doctor and his fourteen-year-old son were elsewhere tending the injured troops, and his wife was home with a newborn. Apparently, the only other child, a six-year-old boy, begged them not to hurt his mom or burn the house and they complied and left. The damage done sometimes depended on the tug at the heartstrings of the men on horseback.

Some troops scattered across Pudding Ridge to Cana where they encountered Lizzy Frost. Rather than a straight line of advancement, soldiers would spread out across farms looking for food and good horses. They were moving to regroup at the county seat of Mocksville. A few dozen men and boys took a position on Bob Wilson Hill outside town in hopes of stopping them. Shots were exchanged, but no defense could be maintained so they ran into the town to warn others. A few Union soldiers wished to

Lee House. *Digital Davie.*

retaliate being shot at by torching the town, but only a cotton mill was burned. Mrs. Braxton Bailey declared that her bed was set on fire after she denied she had any money to surrender to the looters, but exactly why the bed or whether she was in it at the time is lost to history, as is the Lee House, where it happened.

Stoneman was in a hurry to get to Salisbury, so he demanded a quick meal in Mocksville before they moved on, leaving the town frightened but mostly intact. One recollection by S. Oscar Rich told of the Brown Brothers Tobacco factory being threatened. On site was J.F. Pickler, deaf but muscular, who hid the cured tobacco under the porch; the business was salvaged, allowing Brown Brothers to move its operation later to Winston. After food and horses, tobacco was the most desirable loot.

Stoneman's troops went very near Peter Hairston's Cooleemee plantation on their way to Salisbury, never realizing that it was owned by Jeb Stuart's brother-in-law. One of Hairston's slaves slipped away to join the liberators. John Goolsby, the slave who served as the coachman on the plantation, successfully hid the family silver (including some made by Paul Revere).

Brown's Tobacco Factory. *Martin-Wall History Room.*

John Goolsby. *Digital Davie.*

Another plantation slave by the name of Tinker was throwing up breastworks at the Trading Ford; he never could prove his service for a pension with the necessary records, but he did live in freedom until 1932, telling his story.

Citizens of Salisbury were not happy when the state chose an old factory site for a prison camp, positioned right in the heart of downtown, knowing that it would draw enemy fire. It proved the single most important war effort in Salisbury.

The Salisbury prisoner of war camp, the only one in North Carolina, was not always the horrific place it became at the end of the war. In the early years, prisoners were allowed to leave the sixteen acres of the prison camp and roam around downtown Salisbury. On July 4, 1862, Independence Day was celebrated by a parade, a public reading of the Declaration of Independence and other entertainment, including a pig race that the Rebels won when the Yankee-designated pig refused to run (that may have been rigged). There was a friendly game of baseball played between the prison guards and the officers of both sides. Prisoner Otto Boetticher sketched the event in what became one of the earliest renderings of baseball in existence.

When prisoner exchanges stopped for most of 1864, the population in the prison escalated to levels beyond its ability to handle. Originally designed to hold 2,500 to 3,000, it swelled to 10,000. Men were desperately overcrowded, went hungry and were sick and dying.

Historian Louis Brown estimated that four thousand of fifteen thousand housed in the prison died, hastily buried in mass unmarked graves in the

Boetticher's baseball game in Salisbury Prison Camp. *Library of Congress.*

Salisbury National Cemetery. Union states later erected monuments to honor their fallen heroes. Poignant words on these monuments echo: "They banish our anger forever…under the sod and the dew, Awaiting the judgment day, Under the violets the Blue, Under the lilacs the Gray."

Dysentery, smallpox and every other communicable disease ran rampant in the overcrowded conditions. (In fact, more men died in every other aspect of the Civil War than died from battle injuries.) Smallpox victims were treated in separate facilities off the prison camp grounds and buried at the Old Lutheran Cemetery, all in an effort to prevent spread of the disease. Dr. Josephus Hall was the first surgeon at the Salisbury Prison Camp and served there until the very end of the war. Luke Blackmer, an attorney from New York, provided not only books and food to the Union captives but also his barn to hide in when escaping. The Salisbury Prison Camp was in the center of the town, where the citizens were daily engaged in it individually and collectively broken by it.

One surprising death at the Salisbury Prison Camp was the son of legendary missionary David Livingstone (of "Dr. Livingstone, I presume" fame). Livingstone was an outstanding explorer in Africa, a fair missionary and not-so-great family man. His children mostly grew up in Scotland without him for years at a time. After his mother died, teenage Robert joined the U.S. Army under the assumed name of Rupert Vincent (as his father's name was already legendary). He was captured and imprisoned in Salisbury, where as part of an escape attempt Robert was shot and died of his wounds. His hard-to-locate father learned of his death six months later. A local college in Salisbury founded for freed slaves after the war was named for David Livingstone.

The sun rose on the morning of April 12, 1865, to reveal Stoneman's troops lined along Grant's Creek on the outskirts of Salisbury and battle began. General Beauregard, who had worked so diligently to protect the city, had, through serious bungling, been demoted and removed to Greensboro. Troops had also been relocated so Salisbury was defended by about one thousand against Stoneman's four thousand men on horseback. Nonetheless, the defenders made a valiant effort. They dismantled the bridge that spanned the river but within a few hours were pushed back into the city, where civilians panicked. The same day, they learned of Lee's surrender; it all must have seemed so senseless.

General George Stoneman, the wannabe liberator, quickly learned that the prison had been emptied of the final Federal prisoners in one last prisoner exchange. Stoneman and his troops were in Salisbury two days but they managed to burn any building with supply stores, including the old prison buildings, leaving no historical trace of it. Other materials deemed war related were piled on Main Street and set ablaze. Reportedly, the smoke on that night with a nearly full moon could be seen as far away as Statesville and Mocksville. The latter breathed a sympathetic sigh of relief. The former was filled with dread at the sight.

Local merchant Thomas Jefferson Meroney fed Stoneman and his officers an "ample meal" for breakfast in the morning. His hospitality was rewarded when Stoneman interrupted the order to burn the courthouse at T.J.'s pleading. Flames would have quickly spread to Meroney's tobacco warehouse, but he and the county were spared more destruction due to his quick thinking.

Only five days after Stoneman's visit, another guest arrived in Salisbury: Confederate president Jefferson Davis on his escape route. Davis had been sitting in church in Richmond only days before when he was handed a telegram from Robert E. Lee that in more formal military prose could be boiled down to "Run!" After panicking and packing, including $500,000 in gold and the Confederacy currency, he put his wife (with a gun and a hurried lesson in how to load it) and children on a train to Charlotte. He and the cabinet boarded a train headed for Danville, where he very nearly crossed paths with Stoneman and his troops. They torched a train trestle an hour after Davis rode over it; he uttered the words, "A miss is as good as a mile," very optimistic given what lay ahead of him.

The remnant of the Confederate government had been forced to proceed across the Piedmont on horseback with heavy metal currency. It is unclear which route Davis took from Greensboro to Salisbury, but very possibly the back roads would have him and the last remnants of the Confederacy making yet another notable crossing at Shallow Ford, one designed to not draw attention.

Sherman had completed his march and accepted General Johnston's surrender in Raleigh. One Union soldier in Sherman's troops took a souvenir of war with him, the original copy of the Bill of Rights sent to North Carolina in 1789 when it refused to ratify the Constitution without it. It went home (perhaps across the Shallow Ford) with the enemy to Tippecanoe, Ohio, where he sold it for five dollars. Over the next 150 years, the valuable relic changed hands several times (hung in a lawyer's office ironically for a while) and was occasionally offered for sale back to North Carolina. The state always refused, insisting that it was stolen property and still belonged to the State of North Carolina. In just the last 25 years, the Federal Bureau of

Investigation stepped in, confiscating it, and the courts finally ruled that no one was owed compensation for the return to its rightful owner. The Bill of Rights has been back in Raleigh since 2003, righting a wrong from the Civil War 140 years later.

Statesville was Stoneman's next target and suffered the usual fires. One particularly heartbreaking act was the destruction of the newspaper office of the *Iredell Express*. The citizens begged for it to be spared, even offering to dismantle the building themselves and remove the contents; not only was this denied but the questioners were brutally beaten as well.

The raiders continued west to Lenoir and then to Morganton and ultimately to Asheville, which may have been among the last targets in the state but also the hardest hit. George Stoneman meanwhile took a victory lap back through Boone to Knoxville so he could proclaim his victory simultaneously with news of the war ending. The sixty-one-day raid in no way hastened the end of the war, but it greatly demoralized those already beaten down. The raid continued without Stoneman into South Carolina and Georgia in the hopes of catching Jeff Davis, finally limping to a less than glorious finish.

After the raid that gave him the fame he had sought, Stoneman briefly served in the Reconstruction government of Tennessee but his failure to control a riot in Memphis led to him being investigated by Congress. He was reassigned to Arizona but relieved of that command after bungling an Indian massacre. He left military service (with a disability release that President Grant quickly reversed following a public debate as to whether his piles could be considered a battle injury). Finally, he became a one-term governor in California; his term was notable for the many prisoners he pardoned, liberating some prisons at last. While governor, someone burned his house. Lost in the fire were his personal memoirs and war relics, ironic given the many properties he had torched. He died a few years later but his legacy lived on.

The Civil War had come to an end, before Stoneman's Raid did, on April 9 at Appomattox Court House. Lee came to the conclusion that there was no chance of changing the outcome of the war. He and General Ulysses Grant met in the front room of Wilmer McLean's house (the man who famously moved his family south after his farm was overrun in the first Battle of Bull Run, prompting the expression that the war began in his backyard and ended in his front parlor and there was no escaping it). In the end, the terms were generous, as they should be between fellow Americans—soldiers swearing that they would not take up arms against the United States were allowed to go home with their guns and horses needed for plowing that spring. Among these foot soldiers, the Twenty-Eighth North Carolina regiment was represented at Appomattox by 230 men from Yadkin County who started walking home.

The surviving Confederate soldiers began the long trek home, still avoiding crossing paths with the enemy soldiers doing the same. Francis Casstevens wrote the touching story that women put pots of soup out along the road for the hungry soldiers on their way. Many of those weary journeys crossed Shallow Ford on the path home from the horrors of war.

As Jefferson Davis and his cabinet fled south, they carried the Confederate treasury, mostly in gold and silver coins but also jewelry that had been donated to the cause. While some believe its worth was in the millions, it was probably closer to $500,000. The heavy load started out on railcars and then was transferred to slower wagons and packhorses. They had to cross the Yadkin River somewhere and as Trading Ford was a very busy place, the treasury carriers may have taken the backroads using the less traveled Shallow Ford crossing. When the treasury was confiscated by Union forces in Georgia, it was half of what started. Some had been used on the way for supplies and perhaps to buy silence, but persistent tales of portions of it being buried in the North Carolina hinterlands have brought treasure hunters out with metal detectors ever since.

The final cache also disappeared after the escorts were attacked by a band of thieves in Georgia. They made off with what their horses could carry and the remaining coins (reportedly worth about $100,000) were retrieved by a farm family and buried. Being a minister's family, they resisted the urge to take any until the rightful owner could be determined and claim it. That never happened. The general area where it had been buried is now, according to the U.S. Army Corps of Engineers, thirty feet under the flooded area that that makes up Clarks Hill Lake. Water had the final claim on the wealth of the Confederate States of America.

Stoneman's Raid has been given too little attention in Civil War history books, but its memory has lived long in the communities devastated by it. Any discussion should include the resiliency the North Carolinians demonstrated; they never resorted to the scorched-earth response but rather returned to their fields, replanted them and kept on living. Stories of the raid were passed down for the next century about Stoneman's harassment, abuse and robbery. For many, the events of this raid were the worst thing they would ever experience. This author's great-grandmother Jane Stonestreet Boger, in her nineties in the 1960s, retold the stories her mother, Martha Coon

Stonestreet, had told her of hiding and muzzling with her hands the family horses in the woods behind their home when Stoneman's troops marched down Cana Road. Historian James Wall told of how his grandmother Cora Wall hid cured ham above the ceiling, where grease marks showed for years. Almost every family that lived through Stoneman's Raid told stories of hiding, burying or wearing valuable family possessions. Stoneman's legacy was in the oral tradition of his reign of terror.

One interesting form these stories took was captured by The Band (ironically Canadian) in 1969, when Robbie Robertson composed the folk song "The Night They Drove Old Dixie Down" about a fictional Rebel named Virgil Caine whose life was destroyed by Stoneman's Raid. A twentieth-century generation sang:

Virgil Caine is the name
And I served on the Danville train
'Til Stoneman's cavalry came
And tore up the tracks again

In the winter of '65
We were hungry, just barely alive
By May the 10th, Richmond had fell
It's a time I remember, oh so well
The night they drove Old Dixie down...

The most poignant lines were "you take what you need and you leave the rest but they should never have taken the very best." Joan Baez's version took the song to the Top 5 on the pop music charts in 1971 in the United States, the country that won the war.

The former enslaved population struggled to find new means to live with their past. They could teach their neighbors the lyrics "Gonna lay down my burden down by the riverside and I ain't gonna study war no more." One former enslaved woman told her descendants how she stayed alive by eating the leaves on a blackberry bush when suddenly homeless. They rushed to organize their own churches and support systems. Second Presbyterian Church was formed in Mocksville in 1867, meeting first in the sanctuary of First Presbyterian Church, but it had its own building by 1893 along with a school next door for the children of the East Depot neighborhood.

The Civil War forever changed the demographics of the South. North Carolina sent more than 120,000 to serve in the Confederate cause and one-third of them did not return. The war toll of the Civil War was concentrated in young males.

A generation of young men killed in battle was forever lost to future inventions, businesses or political office. Families were devastated and the next generation diminished by the men who did not live to father children. Widows were stranded to sort out life and support children alone. In the nineteenth century, a child was called an orphan if his father died even if the mother still lived, as men provided the economic structure of a family. Millions of young women never married because the men they might have wed did not survive. For the next century, most counties in North Carolina had a county home for the first time, often called the "poor house," populated by handicapped veterans, war widows and spinsters—women for whom the odds were against them and were alone in their old age. The effects of the Civil War extended well into the twentieth century.

It was 24 years before any Civil War pensions were available. Many elderly Confederate veterans married younger women in order to prolong that pension. The last person to ever receive a Civil War pension died of old age in nearby Wilkes County in 2019, 155 years after her father fought in the Civil War. Irene Triplett died at age ninety having received a pension all her life due to disabilities. She could not clearly remember her father, Mose Triplett, but she made history just by living as long as she did. If there were an actual Civil War pension office in Washington, D.C., Irene in a nursing home in Wilkes County was at the end of the line. The financial last chapter of the Civil War ended in the area Stoneman had devastated.

Elizabeth Frost, Lizzybeth earlier in this chapter, not only survived the war in Cana but also lived until 1935, long enough to tell her story of Stoneman's Raid to her granddaughter Annie Laurie Etchinson a few years before the latter became the librarian of the armed forces in World War II. Elizabeth married neighbor and veteran James Harrison Cain. Cain had joined the Confederate navy and was one of only two to escape when the Confederate ram *Albemarle* was torpedoed, but only after Cain destroyed the gun room on board. He swam ashore in the dark of the night with his own muzzle-loading Colt Navy .32-caliber revolver intact. He and Elizabeth lived out their lives in Cana, where he built the Cain Post Office/store, which still stands at the heart of a community that suffered Stoneman's Raid.

One local veteran, Captain Reuben E. Wilson, lost a leg and remained bitter the rest of his life, wearing nothing but his Confederate uniform. The war had not gone well for him and when he was released from prison eight

Elizabeth Frost Cain (*bottom left*) and family in 1898. *Digital Davie.*

months after the war ended, his only other prison mates were Jefferson Davis and John Gee, the last commander at the Salisbury Prison.

One of the last living North Carolina Civil War veterans was a nearly lifelong resident of Hamptonville, Yadkin County, from his birth into slavery in 1842 until his death at age 109 on December 15, 1951. He may also have been the last living former slave who could remember slavery as an adult. Alfred "Teen" Blackburn was enslaved when he accompanied his master, John Augustus Blackburn, as his "body servant" according to his pension which awarded him a Class B pension of $26.26. He had witnessed the First Battle of Bull Run and General Stoneman burning anything in his path in Hamptonville. After the war, Teen tried his hand at mining in Ashe County but quit after one day. He returned to Hamptonville and became a mail carrier, for the next sixty years carrying the mail on foot and later by horse the ten miles from Jonesville to Hamptonville. He and his wife, Lucy, had ten children and farmed a seventy-five-acre tobacco farm in order to give his children a formal education; they, in turn, became teachers, mail carriers and a policeman in the capital city of the United States against whom Teen had been taken to fight so many years before.

Alfred "Teen" Blackburn. *Max Tharpe Collection, Iredell County Public Library.*

The children suffered their own losses. According to the *Yadkin County Heritage Book*, at the height of the Civil War in 1862, in Yadkin County there were seventy schools with more than 1,200 children enrolled and nearly $5,000 was spent on education. From the years 1865 to 1871, no money was available, and public education became practically extinct. The next decade saw a halting effort, with no real education for most children in the county for more than the eleven years a child regularly attended school. Private academies began to spring up after 1880 but there was no regaining lost ground in a child's life.

While the war altered the trajectory of so many lives, it completely changed the arc of ambitions for a grandson of an early setter, telling the story of how one life was derailed by a war. Thomas Lanier Clingman's story had all the elements of the small-town boy who rises to the top except that his chance to be president disappeared before his eyes. Born in the village of Huntsville near the Shallow Ford, he had a pedigree far beyond his humble origins. The descendant of Revolutionary War heroes on both sides, a Presbyterian minister and even the Indian chief Donnahoo, Thomas grew up without a father but was otherwise happy. He loved fishing at the Shallow Ford, even though he nearly drowned on two occasions in the swift-moving water. Thomas received a better than average education and studied law. For one winter, Peter Ney stayed with the family and provided exposure to a bigger world in the backwoods of North Carolina.

Thomas's goal of becoming a great man—and some day president of the United States—began its upward climb. He did a lot of climbing. Clingman relocated his law practice to Asheville and fell in love with the mountains. He explored and measured many peaks, and he may have even determined the highest peak in the eastern United States. While debating this with his former professor, Dr. Elisha Mitchell, the latter fell to his death, and the honor of the highest peak's name went to him. Clingman was given a token prize in Clingmans Dome. His scientific work also included identifying minerals and even later in life competing with Thomas Edison to create the first working lightbulb.

Clingman worked for the railroad to come to the small mountain town of Asheville, and it in return sent Tom to Congress, first to the House of Representatives for two terms, where, not surprisingly, he was an influential voice in the last decade before the slavery issue exploded in civil war. Although he himself never owned a slave and represented a poor mountain area where slavery was rare, he became known as the "Champion of the South" as he defended slave owners' rights and supported secession.

He was first elected to represent the western district in the U.S. Congress in 1842, a year three congressmen who came from Huntsville held national office. Clingman had just been elected to the U.S. Senate when war broke out. Clingman refused to relinquish his seat and was expelled in the end, the last senator from the South to withdraw from the Senate chamber. He had trouble letting go of his dream.

Disappointed that he had been derailed from his government dreams, he organized and led a brigade until he was shot in the leg in August 1864 at Petersburg. He was in Huntsville recovering and hid from Stoneman, who invaded the home of Jane Clingman, Thomas's mother, much like what her mother had endured during the War for Independence in 1781. The general was forced to flee on crutches, lest he be recognized. The women in his family, with the help of slaves, packed up valuables and hid the trunks in the woods, but Stoneman's troops found it all. The 1870 census listed this Clingman household as having "no assets."

As much as Thomas hoped for government office again after the war, his role as an officer in the Confederacy denied him this. He returned to his beloved mountains and promoted tobacco for medicinal purposes. He died in 1897 in the Morganton Hospital for the Insane—the end of an eventful century and a long life that went very differently from what he had wanted.

FINAL CROSSINGS

Ernest Groce and his brother Paul looked forward to skipping school for the overnight trip with their dad from near Harmon Creek to take tobacco to market in Winston-Salem. Driving the mule-drawn Nissen wagon loaded down with the crop took them across the river, heading toward Trade Street on the real tobacco road. An adventure that included a chili supper in a café, a fifteen-cent western movie and camping in the warehouse, where breakfast was cooked over a shared fire, brought excitement even as the sinking prices of tobacco following World War I limited their purchases of long johns at Belk's and food staples at W.G. White's. After laying out the dried tobacco before the buyers, the memory of "watching our hard work being auctioned off" was a rich part of his *Growing Up in Yadkin County*.

Reconstruction had brought northerners to the devastated South and many of them saw the potential. This translated into an injection of money from industries in the North. Railroad tracks, destroyed during the war, were rebuilt and expanded.

Not everyone wanted the railroads; to this day, Yadkin County has almost no (less than a quarter-mile track in the UNIFI factory) railroad tracks in it, after it being considered three times in the late nineteenth century. Davie County, however, welcomed its coming. An article in the newspaper on Valentine's Day 1889 had editor W.X. Coley of the *Davie Times* state that the citizens of Davie are "waiting patiently, as they have done for years, for the iron horse to enter their borders." Train service to Davie County began in 1891. The train went to Winston Salem every morning and returned every

Cooleemee Sunday stroll. *Digital Davie.*

evening, when local residents would turn out to watch. Mail, packages and even animals were unloaded to their delight. It was the evening entertainment for many years.

The Shallow Ford area's economic boom came in tobacco. Smoking had greatly increased demand during the Civil War. An early processor, Major T.J. Brown, began as early as 1858 producing plug tobacco and later moved his business to the town of Winston. Two brothers from Davie County formed the successful Brown Brothers Tobacco Company, at one time the largest and only steam-powered tobacco factory in Winston. Then P.H. Hanes and R.J. Reynolds entered the business in 1874; Brown Brothers merged with Reynolds, which produced the popular chewing tobacco called Brown's Mule after a little mule owned by Thomas Brown (their father) in Mocksville.

Shallow Ford plantation owner John Bitting opened a tobacco factory in Huntsville and later Winston and was a key player in the creation of the Winston Electric Light and Power Company, turning on the streetlights in the city for the first time on the evening of March 25, 1887 (it was a short-lived glow, as a week later a thunderstorm blew out the system and introduced the residents to the concept of an electric surge).

Mocksville Depot at train arrival. *Digital Davie.*

Bitting's daughter Kate married Will Reynolds, who became president of Reynolds Tobacco Company. Will and Kate bought a farm and built a home on land that was already called Tanglewood, south of Shallow Ford, on the Yadkin River, where they lived the rest of their lives. They left it to become a popular park, known for its equestrian and golf activities, as well as the Festival of Lights every year at Christmastime. Kate B. Reynolds, the daughter of a Civil War veteran who never left her humble roots out of her name, made sure that Reynolds money went to many good causes, including bringing Wake Forest University to Winston-Salem and a hospice home bearing her name. She grew up in a Shallow Ford family whom the Civil War left broke and died worth $8 million, much of it donated to help the impoverished of Winston-Salem.

Tobacco provided the perfect business partnership between the factories concentrated around Winston and the outlying farms that grew the crop, evidenced by the many old tobacco barns that dot the area around the Shallow Ford region. Farmers would take farm wagons down cartways and dirt roads, across Shallow Ford, to the warehouses, where they would vie for a place and stack the best grade tobacco leaves they had on top of baskets to be sold.

Tobacco warehouse. *Digital Davie.*

The railroad resurgence and growth facilitated the transportation of the finished tobacco cigars and later cigarettes across the reunited states; smoke-filled back rooms became the new standard in national politics, thanks to Piedmont North Carolina tobacco. By 1888, there were dozens of small tobacco companies in Winston producing brand names such as Free and Easy, Honey Dew, Southern Belle and Brown Jug.

The village of Clemmons south of the Shallow Ford grew from the earliest settlement in 1802 of Peter Clemmons and his family in the homeplace that still stands beside the Clemmons Methodist Church on Highway 158. His descendant Edwin Theodore Clemmons ran a prosperous stagecoach business there as travel increased westward from Winston Salem. He had his stylish stagecoaches custom built, including the one named for his wife, Hattie Butner.

In 1898, Henry Fries utilized the water power of the Yadkin River for a new industry: electric power. Just below Idol's Dam, he harnessed the water for his Idol's Hydroelectric Station, which generated two thousand horsepower in a day. Fries Manufacturing and Power Company was the first in the South to transmit electricity over a long distance, about thirteen miles to a textile plant he owned, reportedly transmitted over barbed wire. Thomas Edison was an investor and visited the site along the banks of the Yadkin.

The best-selling book in the United States in 1901 was a novel called *The Crossing*. It was a sweeping American saga of the young nation during the previous century as it moved into the wide-open West through Kentucky. A journey west began in the Yadkin Valley with, "We crossed the Yadkin at a ford, and climbing the hills to the south of it we went down over stony traces." The book was written by Winston Churchill, not the famous one but an American novelist, who captured the nation's imagination with a real place: Shallow Ford.

History was preserved in 1913 when the Daughters of the American Revolution undertook the mammoth task of determining the path Daniel Boone traveled west in 1769, marking the links that still connect the Forks of the Yadkin to the trans-Appalachian frontier. Twelve permanent markers were cast and deposited beginning at Shallow Ford, where it was bolted onto a rock largely hidden from view, and continued to Zionsville, Tennessee.

The Daniel Boone Heritage Trail was enhanced in 1925 when Davie native J. Hampton Rich voluntarily undertook the project of erecting monuments, many arrowhead shaped. Hampton made it his life's work to

Farmington Boone trail marker. *Keith Hall.*

put more than 250 monuments in place, including one at the Farmington intersection, close to where Daniel Boone left his home on Sugar Tree Creek to head west over Shallow Ford. The North Carolina Daniel Boone Heritage Trail continues to spotlight Boone in the place he loved most: the great outdoors. Thanks to these history savers, moderns can walk in his footsteps or drive the path he blazed across North Carolina into the future.

In the winter of 1939–40, while war loomed in Europe, the Yadkin River froze over and John Stokes Haire of Courtney in Yadkin County told his descendants how he drove a horse and wagon across the ice. Another group cut blocks at Shallow Ford and measured and documented this weather phenomenon. Others spoke of the amazing experience of walking on water if frozen solid in a particularly cold winter.

Ferries still operated until a century ago. Hall's Ferry crossed the Yadkin River for ninety years before the Clemmons Bridge(s). Ferries had rules, including that someone must respond to a summons within fifteen minutes, the summons being a "Wahoo" from the Clemmons side. If the wind was blowing the wrong way, it could not be heard, so a bell was installed. There were rules for the passengers as well, including that they had to drop any traces for horses so if they bolted off the ferry, they would not take the wagon and sink the vessel. High water, deeper than a five-foot rise, stopped the ferry from operating, and farmers transporting tobacco to market took blankets and provisions, as they often had to camp for several days. The river was deeper on the Forsyth side than the Davie, where it was not uncommon for passengers to witness baptisms on Sunday afternoons. (Mr. Cornelius Hall did not like running the ferry on Sunday, but to keep the license, he had to make it available every day.)

The first ferry was made from hewn poplar timbers and measured thirty-seven feet long and fourteen feet wide, big enough for two wagon loads, and required two men to pole it across. The boats had to be replaced every fifteen years, but the cable that cost $150 lasted much longer. The charge for a wagon crossing on the ferry, round trip, was originally forty cents, but the county commissioners reduced it to twenty-five cents. An individual riding was charged a nickel, but the ferryman could double his charge after 9:00 p.m.; it was known that Mr. Hall would not charge preachers. The most frequent passengers were the mail carriers, who used it until 1899 when the mail began to be carried by the trains. There was even a Hall's Ferry Post Office for a while. In spite of having to shut down in winters when the river froze over, running a ferry was a successful business for centuries until it came to an abrupt halt with the automobile and bridges. Hall's Ferry made its final trip across the Yadkin River between Davie County and Clemmons on Easter Monday, 1914.

Sixteen years into the new century, a bridge was built where Hall's Ferry had delivered people across the river. A sign hung on the bridge reading, "No automobiles allowed on bridge while a team is crossing. No team allowed on bridge while an automobile is crossing." Two eras of transportation met but were not allowed to pass each other on this new steel bridge. Even this came at a human cost. A death notice in the *Davie County Record* reported that Charlie Sheek of Farmington "was accidentally killed while working on the new steel bridge across the Yadkin River at Hall's Ferry last Wednesday morning. A part of the bridge on which he was standing fell, and he was precipitated to the ground, the fall breaking his neck. Death was almost instant. Two or three others were slightly injured." When completed, the new bridge was sixteen feet wide and cost $31,000 and one life.

The river saw the biggest changes in how it was crossed. Bridges were nothing new, but they were scarcer in rural areas prior to the Civil War. They had been constructed mostly of wood for centuries—prone to rot, fire and other hazards—but nineteenth-century technology made possible

Hall's Bridge. *Digital Davie.*

iron and then steel bridges, less vulnerable and capable of supporting more weight. The advent of the Industrial Revolution hastened the building of railroad tracks to transport goods and the first bridges were built primarily for train tracks, linking factories with commercial centers. The arrival of the automobile created the demand for bridges with roads, not tracks, across them.

In 1920, a bridge was built just north of the Shallow Ford called West Bend Bridge, ending the common use of Shallow Ford as a river crossing. It can barely be detected from the bridge, if speeding cars allow lingering, lying quietly where it always has.

Shallow Ford almost disappeared in 1936, when the High Point Hydroelectric Project wanted to build a dam at Styers Ferry that would have flooded the whole area below it, including Shallow Ford. However, local farmers sued; the case was fought in the courts for five years and even went to the state supreme court seven times before being ruled in the farmers' favor. According to newspapers, it generated more court documents than any other case in North Carolina history to that time. The Roosevelt administration attempted to revitalize the plan for the war effort but then dropped it. Being left alone by the government is as good as a victory in these parts. Eventually, Lake Norman was created instead and Shallow Ford remains much like it has always been.

In addition to providing drinking water, the Yadkin River also furnishes the counties it courses through with beauty and recreation. The old Shallow Ford on the river will soon be joined to a historic park with paths to walk or bicycle, canoe livery and green space—a place to catch sight of the famous ford after nearly a century of being hidden. Once again, people will see and appreciate its role in shaping history.

Shallow Ford awaits its next chapter as it always has.

CONCLUSION

If a place can be called a National Treasure, this one—Shallow Ford—would certainly qualify. Before there were people or buildings or towns, there was in a river a hidden path just under the surface of the water to help people cross. It was life-changing for many travelers who called a new place home or transported commerce to make a living or went to a "Come to Jesus" meeting. But it also changed the course of history. After the Tories were dispersed by Patriots at Battle Branch and Cornwallis crossed to meet Greene at Guilford Courthouse, the tide turned in the War for Independence and we became Americans. As Stoneman's Raid crossed Shallow Ford, it was determined we would remain Americans. This small watery place became the stage to American history, the way across the river to get to all that lay waiting beyond.

SELECTED BIBLIOGRAPHY

Archives

Davie County Historical and Genealogical Society.
Davie County Public Library, Martin-Wall History Room.
Forsyth County Public Library, North Carolina Room.
Iredell County Historical Society.
Iredell County Library History Room.
Lewisville Historical Society.
Library of Congress.
Rowan County Historical Society.
Rowan Museum Inc.
Wilson Library, University of North Carolina–Chapel Hill.
Wisconsin Historical Society, Draper Manuscript Collections.
Yadkin County Public Library.
Yadkin County Historical and Genealogical Society.
Z. Smith Reynolds Library, Special Collections and Archives, Wake Forest University.

Books

Allen, Thomas B. *Tories: Fighting for the King in America's First Civil War.* New York: HarperCollins, 2010.

Andrlik, Todd. *Reporting the Revolutionary War.* Naperville, IL: Sourcebooks, 2012.

Asbury, Francis. *The Journal and Letters of Francis Asbury*. Vol. 3. Nashville, TN: Abingdon Press, 1958.

Autman, William T. *Civil War in the North Carolina Quaker Belt: The Confederate Campaign Against Peace Agitators, Deserters and Draft Dodgers*. Jefferson, NC: McFarland & Company, 2014.

Bailey, Ralph Edgar. *Guns Over the Carolinas: The Story of Nathanael Greene.* New York: William Morrow and Company, 1967.

Barrett, John G. *The Civil War in North Carolina*. Chapel Hill: University of North Carolina Press, 1963.

Blackwell, Joshua Beau. *The 1865 Stoneman's Raid Begins: Leave Nothing for the Rebellion to Stand Upon.* Charleston, SC: The History Press, 2011.

Blethen, Tyler, and Curtis Wood Jr. *From Ulster to Carolina: The Migration of the Scotch-Irish to Southwestern North Carolina*. Cullowhee, NC: Western Carolina University, 1983.

Brown, Louis A. *The Salisbury Prison: A Case Study of Confederate Military Prisons, 1861–1865*. Wendell, NC: Avera Press, 1980.

Brown, Merrikay Everett, and Darla Morgan Johnson. *Lewisville*. Charleston, SC: Arcadia Publishing, 2002.

Bruce, Dickson D., Jr. *And They Sang Hallelujah: Plain-Folk Camp-Meeting Religion, 1800–1845*. Knoxville: University of Tennessee Press, 1946.

Buchanan, John. *The Road to Guilford Courthouse: The American Revolution in the Carolinas.* New York: John Wiley and Sons, 1997.

Calhoun, Robert M. *Religion and the American Revolution in North Carolina*. Raleigh: North Carolina Department of Cultural Resources, 1976.

Carroll, Grady L.E., ed. *Francis Asbury in North Carolina: The North Carolina Portions of the Journal of Francis Asbury*. Nashville, TN: Parthenon Press, 1964.

Carroll, Henry King. *Francis Asbury in the Making of American Methodism.* New York: Methodist Book Concern, 1923.

Casstevens, Frances H. *The Civil War and Yadkin County, North Carolina.* Jefferson, NC: McFarland & Company, 1997.

———. *Clingman's Brigade in the Confederacy, 1862–1865*. Jefferson, NC: McFarland & Company, 2002.

———. *Tales from the North and the South: Twenty-Four Remarkable People and Events of the Civil War.* Jefferson, NC: McFarland & Company, 2007.

Casstevens, Frances H., ed. *The Heritage of Yadkin County*. Winston-Salem, NC: Hunter Publishing Company, 1981.

Catton, Bruce. *The Civil War.* Boston: Houghton Mifflin, 2005.

Churchill, Winston. *The Crossing*. New York: Macmillan and Company, 1930.

Crow, Jeffrey J., and Larry E. Tise, eds. *The Southern Experience in the American Revolution*. Chapel Hill: University of North Carolina Press, 1978.

Crow, Jeffrey J., Paul D. Escott and Flora J. Hatley. *A History of African Americans in North Carolina*. Raleigh: North Carolina Department of Cultural Resources, 1992.

Davis, Burke. *The Cowpens-Guilford Courthouse Campaign*. Philadelphia: J.B. Lippincott Company, 1962.

Davis, Chester S. *Moravians in Europe and America*. Winston-Salem, NC: Moravia Historical Society, 2000.

Denman, Jeffrey A., and John F. Walsh. *Greene and Cornwallis in the Carolinas: The Pivotal Struggle in the American Revolution, 1780–1781*. Jefferson, NC: McFarland & Company, 2020.

Drake, Richard B. *A History of Appalachia*. Lexington: University of Kentucky Press, 2001.

Draper, Lyman C. *Kings Mountain and Its Heroes*. Reprint. Baltimore, MD: Genealogical Publishing Company Inc., 1971.

Dunaway, Stewart E. *Davie County, N.C.: Road, Bridge and Ferry Records (1836–1909)*. N.p.: self-published, 2013.

Edwards, Morgan. *Materials Towards a History of Baptists in North Carolina*. Philadelphia: American Baptist Historical Society, 1954.

Eskew, Harry, David W. Music and Paul A. Richardson. *Singing Baptists: Studies in Baptist Hymnody in America*. Nashville, TN: Church Street Press, 1994.

Ferguson, Thomas W. *Home on the Yadkin*. Winston-Salem, NC: Clay Printing Company, 1956.

Fischer, Davie Hackett. *Albion's Seed: Four British Folkways in America*. New York: Oxford University Press, 1989.

Fordney, Ben Fuller. *George Stoneman: A Biography of the Union General*. Jefferson, NC: McFarland & Company, 2008.

Franklin, John Hope, and Alfred A. Moss Jr. *From Slavery to Freedom: A History of African Americans*. New York: Alfred A. Knopf, 1994.

Fries, Adelaide, Stuart Thurman Wright and J. Edwin Hendricks. *Forsyth: The History of a County on the March*. Chapel Hill: University of North Carolina Press, 1976.

Fries, Adelaide, trans. *The Records of the Moravians*. Raleigh: North Carolina Historical Commission, 1968.

Gerard, Philip. *The Last Battleground: The Civil War Comes to North Carolina*. Chapel Hill: University of North Carolina Press, 2019.

Golway, Terry. *Washington's General: Nathanael Greene and the Triumph of the American Revolution*. New York: Henry Holt and Company, 2006.

Grissom, W.L. *History of Methodism in North Carolina*. Nashville: Publishing House of the M.E. Church, South, 1905.

Groce, Ernest Clarence, and Barbara Nuzum Groce. *Growing Up in Yadkin County, NC and Other Family Stories*. N.p.: self-published, 2016.

Hairr, John. *Guilford Courthouse: Nathanael Greene's Victory in Defeat March 15, 1781*. Cambridge, MA: Da Capo Press, 2002.

———. *North Carolina Rivers: Facts, Legends and Lore*. Charleston, SC: The History Press, 2007.

Hall, William James, and Helen Johnson McMurray. *Tanglewood: Historic Gem of Forsyth County, North Carolina*. Winston-Salem, NC: Hunter Publishing Company, 1979.

Hammon, Neal O., ed. *My Father, Daniel Boone: The Draper Interviews with Nathan Boone*. Lexington: University Press of Kentucky, 2012.

Hartley, Chris J. *Stoneman's Raid, 1865*. Winston-Salem, NC: John H. Blair, 2010.

Hasty, Mary Alice, and Hazel M. Winfree. *The Civil War Roster of Davie County, North Carolina*. Jefferson, NC: McFarland & Company, 2009.

Heimert, Alan. *Religion and the American Mind: From the Great Awakening to the Revolution*. Cambridge, MA: Harvard University Press, 1966.

Hendricks, Garland A. *Saints and Sinners at Jersey Settlement*. Lexington, NC: Jersey Baptist Church, 1964.

Howard, David. *Lost Rights: The Misadventures of a Stolen American Relic*. Boston: Mariner Books, 2010.

Jeffrey, Thomas E. *Thomas Lanier Clingman: Fire Eater from the Carolina Mountains*. Athens: University of Georgia Press, 1998.

Jonas, W. Glenn, Jr., ed., for the North Caroliniana Society. *Religious Traditions of North Carolina, Histories, Tenets and Leaders*. Jefferson, NC: McFarland & Company, 2018.

Jones, Randell. *Before They Were Heroes at Kings Mountain*. Winston-Salem, NC: Daniel Boone Footsteps, 2011.

Kars, Marjoleine. *Breaking Loose Together: The Regulator Rebellion in Pre-Revolutionary North Carolina*. Chapel Hill: University of North Carolina Press, 2002.

Keever, Homer M. *Iredell, Piedmont County*. Statesville, NC: Brady Printing Company, 1976.

Konstam, Angus. *Guilford Courthouse, 1781: Lord Cornwallis' Ruinous Victory*. Oxford, UK: Osprey Publishing, 2002.

Lawson, John. *Lawson's History of North Carolina*. Richmond, VA: Garrett and Massie, 1937.

Lefler, Hugh, ed. *North Carolina History Told by Contemporaries*. Chapel Hill: University of North Carolina Press, 1934.

Little, Lewis Peyton. *Imprisoned Preachers and Religious Liberty in Virginia*. Lynchburg, VA: J.P. Bell Company, 1938.

Lossing, Benson. *The Pictorial Field-Book of the Revolution*. Vol. 2. Rutland, VT: Charles E. Tuttle Company, 1972.

Lumpkin, William L. *Baptist History in the South*. St. John, IN: Larry Harrison, 1995.

Maass, John R. *The Battle of Guilford Courthouse*. Charleston, SC: The History Press, 2020.

Messick, Hank. *King's Mountain: The Epic of the Blue Ridge "Mountain Men" in the American Revolution*. Boston: Little, Brown and Company, 1976.

Miller, Perry. *Errand into the Wilderness*. Cambridge, MA: Belknap Press of Harvard University, 1956.

Morgan, Robert. *Boone: A Biography*. Chapel Hill, NC: Algonquin Books of Chapel Hill, 2007.

Morrill, Dan. *The Civil War in the Carolinas*. Charleston, SC: Nautical and Aviation Publishing Company of America, 2002.

Nash, Gary B. *The Unknown American Revolution: The Unruly Birth of Democracy and the Struggle to Create America*. New York: Viking, 2005.

Paine, Robert. *Life and Times of William McKendree*. Nashville, TN: Methodist Episcopal Publishing House, 1922.

Pancake, John S. *This Destructive War: The British Campaign in the Carolinas, 1780–1782*. Tuscaloosa: University of Alabama Press, 1985.

Paschal, George Washington. *History of North Carolina Baptists*. Vol. 2. Raleigh: North Carolina Baptist State Convention, 1955.

Phillips, Marcia D. *Davie County Mavericks*. Charleston, SC: The History Press, 2018.

Phillips, Ulrich Bonnell. *Life and Labor in the Old South*. Boston: Little, Brown, and Company, 1929.

Powell, William S. *North Carolina: A History*. Chapel Hill: University of North Carolina, 1977.

Ramsey, Robert W. *Carolina Cradle, Settlement of the Northwest Carolina Frontier, 1747–1762*. Chapel Hill: University of North Carolina Press, 1964.

Raynor, George. *Patriots and Tories in Piedmont Carolina*. Salisbury, NC: Salisbury Printing Company, 1990.

Reynolds, G. Galloway. *The Shallow Ford* and *Shallow Ford Country*. Lewisville, NC: self-published, 1992.

Ridgway, Richard. *Self-Sufficiency at All Costs: Confederate Post Office Operations in North Carolina, 1861–1865*. Charlotte: North Carolina Postal History Society, 1988.

Rogers, Floyd, and Douglas L. Rights. *Yadkin Passage and a Voyage Down the Yadkin–Great PeeDee River*. Winston-Salem, NC: Winston-Salem Journal, 1983.

Rohrer, S. Scott. *Hope's Promise: Religion and Acculturation in the Southern Backwoods*. Tuscaloosa: University of Alabama Press, 2005.

Rosenberg, Bruce A. *Can These Bones Live?: The Art of the American Folk Preacher*. Urbana: University of Illinois Press, 1970.

Rouse, Parke, Jr. *The Great Wagon Road, from Philadelphia to the South*. Richmond, VA: Dietz Press, 2016.

Rumple, Jethro. *A History of Rowan County, North Carolina*. Baltimore, MD: Regional Publishing Company, 1974.

Russell, David Lee. *The American Revolution in the Southern Colonies*. Jefferson, NC: McFarland & Company, 2000.

Sabin, Edwin L. *Kit Carson Days, 1809–1868*. Lincoln: University of Nebraska Press, 1995.

Schweiger, Beth Barton. *A Literate South: Reading Before Emancipation*. New Haven, CT: Yale University Press, 2019.

Schweiger, Beth Barton, ed. *Religion in the American South*. Chapel Hill: University of North Carolina Press, 2004.

Shirley, Michael. *From Congregation Town to Industrial City: Culture and Social Change in a Southern Community*. New York: New York University Press, 1994.

Southern, Ed, ed. *Voices of the American Revolution in the Carolinas*. Winston-Salem, NC: John F. Blair, 2009.

Sparks, John. *The Roots of Appalachian Christianity*. Lexington: University Press of Kentucky, 2001.

Stephenson, Michael. *Patriot Battles: How the War of Independence Was Fought*. New York: HarperCollins, 2007.

Stimson, R. Kyle. *The Great Philadelphia Wagon Road in Forsyth County, N.C., 1750–1770*. Lewisville, NC: self-published, 1999.

Thane, Elswyth. *The Fighting Quaker: Nathanael Greene*. New York: Hawthorn Books, 1972.

Thayer, Theodore. *Nathanael Greene: Strategist of the American Revolution*. New York: Twayne Publishers, 1960.

Tise, Larry E. *The Yadkin Melting Pot: Methodism and the Moravians in the Yadkin Valley, 1750–1850*. Winston-Salem, NC: Clay Printing Company, 1967.

Tocqueville, Alexis de. *Democracy in America*. Translated by Henry Reeve. New York: Adlard and Saunders, 1838.
Trotter, William R. *Bushwhackers: The Civil War in North Carolina the Mountains*. Winston-Salem, NC: John F. Blair, 1988.
Tursi, Frank V. *Winston-Salem: A History*. Winston-Salem, NC: John F. Blair Publishers, 1994.
Van Noppen, Ina Woestemeyer. *Stoneman's Last Raid*. Raleigh: North Carolina University, 1961.
Wall, James. *History of Davie County*. Mocksville, NC: Davie County Historical Association, 1969.
Ward, H. Trawick. *Time Before History: The Archaeology of North Carolina*. Chapel Hill: University of North Carolina Press, 1999.
Watt, W.N. *The Granville District*. Taylorsville, NC: self-published, 1992.
Weslager, C.A. *The Log Cabin in America, from Pioneer Days to the Present*. New Brunswick, NJ: Rutgers University Press, 1969.
White, Kevin, and the Clemmons Historical Society. *Clemmons*. Images of America series. Charleston, SC: Arcadia Publishing, 2013.
Wiley, C.H. *North Carolina Reader, Number III*. New York: A.S. Barnes & Company, 1868.
Williams, Juan, and Quinton Dixie. *This Far by Faith; Stories from the African American Religious Experience*. New York: William Morrow, 2003.

Online Sources

digitalnc.org.
https://docsouth.unc.edu/csr.
ncdanielboonetrail.org.
ncpedia.org.
wikipedia.org.

Unpublished Primary Sources

Brumfield, Lewis Shore. "Thomas Lanier Clingman and the Shallow Ford Families." Yadkinville, NC, n.d.
Casstevens, Frances Harding. "The Legends of Huntsville." Yadkinville, NC, 1976.

Curtis, Ed, ed. *The Prison Exchange*. Newsletter produced by the Salisbury Confederate Prison Association, Salisbury, NC, 2020–21.

Forsyth County Historic Resources Commission. "Forsyth County Phase Two Survey Update Report." Winston-Salem, NC, 2008.

Lindsay, Marcellene Blackburn, and Wanda Carter Craaybeek. "People of Color of Yadkin County, North Carolina." Yadkin Historical and Genealogical Society, Yadkinville, NC, 1992.

McMurtry, David C. "Colonel Jonathan Hunt 1716–1782 and Some of His Antecedents and Descendants." Lexington, KY, Mil-Mac, 2012.

McMurtry, David C., David R. Bryan, Kathryn Weiss, John K. Bryan Jr. and Pat R. Forbis. "Seven Sons and Two Daughters of Morgan Bryan (1671–1763), 'Irish Immigrant' and Some of Their Descendants." Lexington, KY, 2009.

McMurtry, David Cornelius, David Randall Bryan and Kathryn Horton Weiss, comps. "Morgan Bryan (1671–1763): A Danish-Born Irish Immigrant and Some of His Antecedents and Descendants." Lexington, KY, 2007.

Weiss, Kathryn. "Morgan Bryan Senior's 'Original Eleven,' Anson (Rowan) County, North Carolina Granville Land Grants." N.d.

West, Betty Etchison. "Cana Connections." Cana, NC, 2011.

Williams, Lewis James, III, Joseph Lanier Williams, Rebecca Turner Williams and Lewis Lanier Williams, comps. "Williams, 300 Years of Leadership in America." Lewisville, NC, 1997.

INDEX

S

T

W

Y

ABOUT THE AUTHOR

The author of *Davie County Mavericks*, historian Marcia D. Phillips works in the Martin-Wall History Room in the Davie County Public Library and also as a history and preservation freelancer. She can be contacted or resourced at www.marciadphillips.com.